In the Spirit

In the Spirit

Steven DeLay

CHRISTIAN ALTERNATIVE
BOOKS

Winchester, UK
Washington, USA

JOHN HUNT PUBLISHING

First published by Christian Alternative Books, 2021
Christian Alternative Books is an imprint of John Hunt Publishing Ltd.,
No. 3 East St., Alresford, Hampshire SO24 9EE, UK
office@jhpbooks.com
www.johnhuntpublishing.com
www.christian-alternative.com

For distributor details and how to order please visit the 'Ordering' section on our website.

Text copyright: Steven DeLay 2020

ISBN: 978 1 78904 753 0
978 1 78904 754 7 (ebook)
Library of Congress Control Number: 2021930252

A CIP catalogue record for this book is available from the British Library.

Design: Stuart Davies

UK: Printed and bound by CPI Group (UK) Ltd, Croydon, CR0 4YY
Printed in North America by CPI GPS partners

We operate a distinctive and ethical publishing philosophy in
all areas of our business, from our global network of authors to
production and worldwide distribution.

Contents

Chapter 1

A Drunkard's Sleep

"Am I in darkness?"

To put this question to ourselves, seriously so, is to place ourselves in question, or better, to come to recognize that we already were, for in interrogating ourselves explicitly in this way, we realize that life itself is an examination, a realization whereby we experience the weight of our always already having been seen by God. Whether in response we in turn treat God as a friend or an enemy remains ours to decide, but ignoring the fact that such a decision must be made is no longer feasible. This moment is one of reckoning, an awakening, a rupture in time revealing that everything preceding it was simply a prelude, a stretch of existence, however long it lasted, now disclosed to have been a state of insensibility. Once eternity has interdicted us, everything is changed forever.

With this awakening comes the awareness that the life which had come before is something to be likened to a drunkenness, or even a sleep. Like a lie, so too drunkenness refuses what it promises. Promising rest, it produces more of the same unease responsible for having led its victim to seek escape in the first place. And, sometimes, as the empty oblivion of a night's fleeting revelry attests, the cure is worse than the illness. For as anyone who follows its path to the bitter end comes to know, this is a way of disappointment only. Staging the allure of peace, drunkenness instead repays nothing but agitation and restlessness. To take one telling example of where its path leads, consider the figure of the drunken sleeper. Where has our sleeper found himself? Ensnared by the tantalizing promise of intoxication's escape, now here he lies swindled into a restless, failed sleep. His body bears witness to the plunge's futility. This is not the release the sleeper sought. We see a painful reminder that such escape remains an unfulfilled hope. And the form this sleep's failure assumes is evident, perhaps above all, when it at its deepest. The snores of one passed out only enforce the impression, as anyone still awake in the room listening will attest, that the rest the sleeper desires is eluding him. Often, we cannot easily wake the drunken from their sleep. But this merely underscores the sleep's inner fitfulness. Even an unresponsiveness may conceal a fury. This storm raging within the sleeper explains why nobody, not even the one who has become accustomed to a life of overindulgence's subtle charms, has ever emerged from a night of drunken sleep feeling truly refreshed. The drunk sleep in vain.

Is it incidental, then, that at the beginning of a reflection concerning the spiritual significance of drunkenness, we should find ourselves led to the consideration of sleep? What secret does the relationship between them contain? By appreciating how each implicates the other, would we not thereby be groping toward, however remote a thing it may appear initially, the question of faith? Or better, by exploring the symbolic significance of drunkenness as a form of spiritual sleep, are we not led to the recognition of faith's very absence?

The first noteworthy thing about the connection between drunkenness and bad sleep is that, although no one disputes it, many nevertheless persist in disregarding this connection. Many, after all, plunge themselves willfully into inebriation knowing well the consequences doing so entails. But if they are willing to take most other necessary precautions to guard against a bad night's sleep, exercising every ritual they have been taught will do so, why is avoiding drunkenness the exception to that rule? Why does it find a place in one's bedtime preparations? Why are there those, who, prepared to do basically anything to avoid a poor night's sleep, get drunk just before nodding off? A drunken stupor makes for a bad night's rest, yet this does not dissuade them from drinking. At the level of contradictory desire, here the everyday connection between sleep and drunkenness is unmistakable even if (or rather exactly because) a night of heavy drinking hampers the sleep it induces. The association between sleep and drunkenness is all the more evident when one notes how the latter is capable of ushering in a form of extreme insensibility unparalleled by anything besides dreamless sleep. This is why, just as the sober melancholic is prone to drowning his sorrows through oversleeping, so too the drunkard is prone to drowning his own in the bottle. Sometimes, in a cry for help brought to perfection, one achieves an almost incessant state of insensibility. Drinking by day, sleeping at night, the one escape segues with seamless transition into the other, producing an uninterrupted cycle of unconsciousness. And if, as the melancholic learns, the escape of an ordinary night's sleep is incapable of dulling the ache of living, then, as the drunkard knows, there always is the consolation of being able to turn by day to the comforts of the bottle, of what is on ice. The drink opens a wayward panacea, lightening our daily burdens that no dark slumber, however temporarily satisfying, ever will. Drinking, in short, becomes a way of sleepwalking through the day.

For this reason, drunkenness itself is a kind of lucid dreaming. Dostoevsky emphasized the point in *Crime and Punishment* when, portraying Raskolnikov's precipitous descent into anguish after having committed murder, the passersby that he encounters on the St. Petersburg streets mistake his spiritual delirium for drunkenness. As is well known, and as the novel's wrenching descriptions of the city's grimy taverns make clear, often this kind of sleepwalking, as it were, assumes a collective effort. It is a joint undertaking, a collaborative illusion requiring the participation of many dreamers, each as unwilling as the others to be alone with the truth. No less than the intoxicating power of the drink itself, just as essential to sustaining the illusion of happiness is a consoling presence that affirms (and is careful never to challenge) its pretense. Nothing, in fact, can be more beguiling than the drinking buddies who form a permanent fixture down at the neighborhood watering hole. Without them there waiting to sustain the dream's intoxication, one might awake, and the dream would evaporate.

The resulting scene is as dejecting as it is typical of such places. Adriaen van Ostade's *Drunkards in a Tavern* (1640) captures it well. Before us is a profound, heavy sadness. That none of the three men in the dingy tavern are able to tolerate being alone with themselves is the first clue that this boisterous tavern is not the happy place they would have us believe. Misery loves company, to be sure, yet sometimes the fact goes underappreciated that this is so all the more when such misery has resolved to try to convince anyone who will listen to it that it is happy. The drinkers become actors, hoping their feigned merriment will pass for the sincere joy they wish was theirs, but is not. Joy experiences contentment in solitude. Here, by contrast, are three men who will do anything to elude being alone.

Looking closely, a crack in this kind of jovial veneer is bound to appear. Ostade's tavern is no exception. Despite their valiant efforts (the many varieties of which Ostade shows beautifully), the room's boisterousness fails to conceal, much less dispel, the men's sorrow. The faces of these reputed free-spirits show so. While it is possible for someone to play at just about anything, these men know inside there is no avoiding what the glassy sheen of a distant stare reveals to others. The room is draped in sadness. And they feel it. Take, for instance, the man in the foreground's right. Sitting disconnected from the shenanigans, his forlorn look mirrors the despondence his two friends are busy trying to silence. In a moment of listless honesty, he is unable to muster so much as a smile. If this man's dejection is apparent, it is because his posture expresses desperate isolation (elbow on knee, the gaze fixed firmly on nowhere). But it is also evident in the manner by which his friends choose to carry themselves in such striking contrast. See, first, the man on the far left's gestures, whose broad mannerisms reproduce the opposite impression of his sullen and shrunken companion. Rather than staring into oblivion as the listless man is, he has devised a strategy to ward off the despair, focusing his attention on his friend as a distraction. Looking for reassurance, he is met with a look that is seeking to do the same. In this crossing of the gazes, both men are able to suppress the realization a look at the room around them would induce. Nonetheless, the sadness seeps in. It is a sadness threatening to cross over into pure desperation when, as we notice, the same man's outstretched arm clutching the hem of the middle figure's shirt, a sign he's grasping for anything (his hat appears to have been plucked off his head by the man in the middle) that might keep him from descending into the despair that has already overtaken the pensive man on the right. When in dire straits as these, sometimes a thing so meagre as a shirt can play the role of a lifeline.

But if this game of diversion is to succeed, it must sustain itself. After all, it's is a sophisticated production demanding careful oversight. There must be someone, then, who is willing to orchestrate everything. And who is the maestro of our little performance but the man positioned directly in the middle? Standing tall, he presides over the fleeting affair with the bravado of a conductor perched over his orchestral pit. Noticing that he has just lost the attention of the sitting man to his left, and sensing that the man to his right could be next, he redoubles his efforts to keep the latter under his spell. And so he must, for it is only by amusing others that he avoids having to confront his own trial of solitude. For as long as he occupies the center of somebody's attention, he won't have to face any unwelcome thoughts regarding the ugly truths waiting to intrude themselves. In the resulting game of playacting, each knows as well as the other it is easier to sustain an illusion when it is collective. Ostade's tavern, we see, has become a theater stage. In unspoken cahoots with each other, our two "happy" drunkards play their role, reassuring themselves that everything is well and fine, so that nobody has to confront the sadness stalking them. There is every reason to surmise, however, as Ostade suggests with the blotted faces of those in the background, that the men's superficial euphoria will soon wane. Sooner than any of them would like, a silence will fall upon their gathering, as it already has the individual man on the right. And with the gap of silence in the noisy banter, our revelers will be left facing the sad reality of things. If playing at being content can only work for so long, then in deciding to cast them in lighting reminiscent of the stage spotlight, Ostade does well to emphasize the theatricality of the tavern spectacle. As if we were peering through the tavern's door before wisely choosing to pass on by, we see this is not the delightful place our three drunkards would like to pretend that it is.

Sight of Ostade's tavern evokes the thought of a spiritual crisis. These men are in peril. That our thought turns inevitably in that direction is unsurprising, especially when one considers the scene in light of the biblical understanding of drunkenness, which often associates drunkenness with sleep, something which for its own part functions as a metaphor for faithlessness. As for our tavern, it unquestionably is the scene of an empty vigil. Waiting on nothing, the men are lost. For what are they seeking in each other's company but a contentment they will not find? The liquid on tap is incapable of quenching a spiritual thirst only the living water can, the water, in short, as we shall see soon, of which Christ speaks of at the well. Thus, even in denying the existence of this thirst afflicting him, the drunkard on the right who has come to the tavern knowing he will find only more misery, is so disconsolate and detached. This daily pilgrimage, he knows, must end in thirst. It is unpleasant to be parched with a carnal thirst, but worse still is the thirst of the spirit, one that remains no matter how much one drinks. Although they dare not say so to the others, the men know what they drink cannot solve the predicament they are facing. They are thirsty, and thirsty with a thirst that no beer can quench.

It is a testament to the power of Ostade's vision that he underscores the scene's theatricality by saturating the figures in a halo of light reproducing conditions not actually feasible till centuries later with the invention of electricity. Appearing precisely where it shouldn't, from above, the interior's light illuminates the figures in a spotlight underscoring that these actors are deceived. But the light indicates even more. A first clue that it does has been noted, albeit in passing. Strictly speaking, the light's shining where it does is a natural impossibility. It descends from above on our figures, illuminating them in a focal spotlight, yet without any discernible candle (much less lightbulb!) to which one could identify the source. What then, the question becomes, is the source? Having ruled out any apparently natural hypothesis, we must conclude that this light, shining as it does, is intended to be symbolic, attesting to the supernatural presence of invisible heights. Depicting a light where it should not be, Ostade suggests that even in the most wretched of places the heavenly light shines. The fact those living enshrouded in such darkness fail to notice the light's presence does not change that they are moving beneath it. In fact, far from their obliviousness being unexpected, the men's ignorance of the light only underscores its presence. In a place as insignificant as a squalid tavern, we see, in Ostade's rendering, an extraordinary event owing to the spiritual light illuminating it. The setting in which these drunkards move is nothing short of supernatural, though the men know it not. The Johannine formula is fulfilled: "And the light shineth in darkness; and the darkness comprehended it not" (John 1:5).

How their plight is as quotidian as it is spiritual comes

further into view the moment the thirst Ostade is depicting is understood to be a yearning for rest, for peace. This thirst for rest thirsts for a contentment eluding us in the time leading to death. Why, then, think it may ever be found in a tavern? Of course, it cannot. As it happens, no place can provide it. There is no destination, however remote or exotic, that delivers it. In trooping down to the tavern, our revelers are simply an obvious reminder of why this truism holds. They desire a rest drunkenness cannot provide. If Ostade shows magnificently how the men seek to quench a thirst that no tavern carousing can, it is only because, as each of us knows for ourselves, they are suffering from a thirst nothing on earth can slake.

The rest we truly need, Ostade suggests, is accordingly heavenly. A way to show so is to reveal, as the sad tavern does, a common way people seek it, yet fail to find it—by drinking at the tavern. There is a similar futility in trying to manufacture it in all of the other various ways people do. If, with Aristophanes, we may say that something has split each of us in two (wholeness now consigned to an immemorial past), it falls to love to somehow restore us to whatever extent that will be possible. Yet not just any love will do. Far from making us whole again, some loves only worsen the estrangement we were trying to overcome, deepen the wounds we have already suffered—a love of the bottle is one of these. Socrates is known to have been the occasional binge drinker, to be sure. Yet, as Plato reports in the *Symposium*, though Socrates drank, he somehow never became drunk. So while we do not know what Socrates was hoping to achieve by drinking (apparently it was not the euphoria of intoxication), we know it was not escape he sought. The restlessness of existence burdened him like every mortal, yet he accepted Ostade's lesson that drinking is no cure for it.

A considerable portion of daily life is a struggle against such restlessness. The task is to somehow shoulder it without thereby allowing it to crush us under its weight. And the danger is heightened by the fact that, although bad habits are our own, it remains the case that, from the biblical perspective, there are powerful dark forces intensifying that struggle by further tempting us. Why drunkenness is prone to boil into violence attests to these powers of strife arrayed against us. When it erupts, one can trace the drunkard's rage to a frustration originating in the unquenchable thirst for peace he cannot find. As drunken brawls attest, drinking often renders some unable to control themselves. There are powerful emotions swirling beneath the banalities of whatever circumstances that incite the fury. Strong drink will sometimes make someone rage, but when the rage erupts, does not the irruption go to show the rage was always already there? It was simmering. As Adriaen Brouwer's *Peasants Brawling over Cards* (1630) and *Tavern Scene* (1635) illustrate, frivolities can trigger fierce violence from those, who, having given into the temptation of drinking in order to forget their pain and frustration, find themselves succumbing to the next temptation that comes their way. As Brouwer shows, the fuse can be as trivial as a disagreement over a game of cards. Drunkenness exacerbates a wrath that, ever latent, now explodes.

The morning after a drunken bout of senseless rage, it is tempting to deal with the shame one feels by focusing on what one did, not the fact that the drunkenness leading there is itself bad, too. To think this way is pure fantasy. Even if someone were to clinicalize the matter by interpreting alcoholism as a disease, the act of drunkenness, from the biblical perspective, remains a moral wrong. The Bible's moral vignettes, which today are often ignored by those who think they know better than to concern themselves with what the Bible says, insist that if we sweep aside the testimony of conscience, we only do so at our own peril. After all, one feels badly about oneself after having done foolish things while drinking, because what one did is not just embarrassing, but wrong. As an example, we might consider Noah's own wine-induced mishap, which is recounted in Genesis, and reproduced in Bellini's 1515 *Drunkenness of Noah*.

When his sons discover Noah asleep naked, the shame they feel for him has less to do with any social embarrassment (considerable as it may be) owing to their seeing their father exposed. More to the point, the shame of the situation consists in the disappointment over a father, who, until then, had been righteous, even spotless. The sordidness has less to do with the nakedness itself, more with the drunkenness responsible for bringing it to be. The Genesis narrative, in fact, by emphasizing the shame of the nakedness, in turn highlights the severity of the transgression by attributing it to drunkenness, and not some other cause. It is not that Noah bears too much simply in the sense of literal nakedness, but that he bears witness to the very sin, and thus the weakness of heart, preceding it. We do not know precisely how Noah met the dawn (the narrative does not say), but there is nothing preventing us from surmising that the grief he felt probably was concerned less with being seen naked by his sons, and instead more so over the spectacle that he had made of himself, a situation that was the natural, but avoidable, consequence of his decision to have plunged himself there. Noah, in keeping with his usually upright behavior, we may imagine, likely mourned over the inner ugliness of the drunkenness itself, not so much the intersubjective indelicacies that followed after because of it.

The intrinsic ignominy of drunkenness arises in other contexts, too. Is it not the case, for instance, that perhaps nothing perturbs those swept up in the enthusiasm of revelry more than an encounter with a sober outsider? Without a spoken word being uttered, this unintoxicated other, simply by his mere presence, convicts them. What makes Ham's reaction to his father's plight so distasteful, then, is not just the cruelty of choosing to ridicule someone he loves in a moment of the beloved's moral weakness, but that he delighted in the knowledge that Noah, who was formerly blameless, was in a way now no better than he. Ham's response to Noah's personal fall is instructive, because it is generalizable. Though it is known that many secretly hate a do-gooder, it is precisely because those who despise good already hate themselves. Ham, in short, was happy to see Noah join the crowd of those who already had found something about themselves to loathe.

Our analysis to present must now face an objection. For will not someone claim that what has been said is nothing more than moralizing? Drunkenness leads to a host of misdeeds, the objection begins, but that, so it continues, merely shows that what one does while drunk is perhaps worthy of our disapproval, though the drunkenness itself deserves no similar censure. To insist, as we have, that drunkenness is not just a moral failing, but a spiritual one also, strike's the modern secular sensibility as too much. And in any case, although no one denies the connection between drunkenness and violence, sexual indiscretion, vehicular homicide, and other evils, have we really gone any way to showing that in drunkenness we are truly dealing with the antipode of faith?

Here, the biblical texts are instructive. In his first letter to those at Corinth, for example, Paul observes the power and the hope which the Resurrection unfurls. As Emmanuel Falque has shown in *The Metamorphosis of Finitude*, it changes everything.[1] To begin with, as Paul clarifies, the Corinthians now have two alternatives between which they must choose. The first option, naturally known to all, lies outstretched before anyone who decides to lay his hope in the material comforts of the time that leads to death. This path, he explains, is one of a hedonism that must keep at bay its underlying hopelessness. Death, for it, is the end. Hence, all that remains for this materialism to do is to eat and drink: "What advantageth it me, if the dead rise not? Let us eat and drink; for tomorrow we die" (1 Cor. 15:32). Far from entailing just a hangover, however, a night's drinking puts out the spirit. The one who overindulges dulls his sensibility to a life that has otherwise become intolerable, one that, in having refused to turn its attention to spiritual things, has exhausted the fire for anything higher than the carnal. It is a recipe for despair: "Who hath woe? Who hath sorrow? Who hath contentions? Who hath babbling? Who hath wounds without cause? Who hath redness of eyes?" (Prov 23:29). Bitten by the serpent, stung by the adder, those who indulge the cravenness of drinking culture stoke a dependency, not on a chemical substance only, but a despondency from which they eventually come to see as having no escape. As the same stretch of the Proverbs just quoted continues a few lines later: "Yea, thou shalt be as he that lieth down in the midst of the sea, or as he that lieth upon the top of a mast" (Prov 23:34). Adrift without destination, one is hurled upon the same bottle never delivering.

Today, it is common to see discounted the matter's spiritual dimension as described by Paul. For no matter how profound or incontestable that dimension may be, and no matter how clearly the letters of the Hebrew prophets and early Christians analyze it, the wisdom of these texts is frequently ignored. Undeterred, there are many who continue to pursue the vanity of worldly pleasures, thinking they somehow will find peace. The mistake of doing so was not apparent to those seeing things from the Hebraic perspective alone. Others, Greek or Roman included, have remarked on this folly too. On the subject of earthly delights, Seneca, for one, casts the same verdict as Paul. Carnal things are unable to satisfy us, he says, for, "if they could ever satisfy us, they would have done so by now."[2] And how could it escape anyone's attention that, in noting this vanity of earthly pleasures, Seneca uses sleep as the metaphor for the condition of those who cling to such things? As he saw well, the insensibility of sleep may afflict someone during the light of day as much as it does in the dead of night. In fact, the greatest danger is to fall into a sleep in which one forgets one is even sleeping. As Seneca states, "a person sleeping lightly perceives impressions in his dreams and is sometimes, even, aware during sleep that he is asleep," but there is a kind of sleep, one more pernicious than this first, one that "blots out even dreams and plunges the mind too deep for consciousness of self."[3] In dreamless sleep such as this, one is nowhere, which is why Seneca describes it aptly when he characterizes it is as an obliviousness to oneself and one's true condition. Life becomes a sleepwalking enslaved to the pursuit of empty comforts. And it gets worse for the sleeper. For in order to pry oneself from this condition, one must first admit that one is a victim of it, but it is this very admission the condition itself renders so difficult. When asleep like this, one is insensible to the fact of one's sleeping: "Why does no one admit his failings? Because he's still deep in them. It's the person who's awakened who recounts his dream, and acknowledging one's failings is a sign of health."[4] Seneca's implicit question is a serious one. How do we awake from a dream, when it is our waking life from which we must awake?

If drunkenness is underpinned by carnal hopelessness, and hence leads to spiritual numbness, it remains to be shown how the alternative course proposed to the Corinthians by Paul differs. How, exactly, does one walk this other way? What is this way of the Spirit? First, it is a way open to everyone. One simply must be willing to seek it, if one is to in turn follow it. The life of the Spirit requires a resolution to break from the carnal course of focusing exclusively on matters concerning our being-in-the-world. Eternity must enter the frame. But here, a doubt inserts itself naturally: is not the futility of a life of eating and drinking unsurpassable? Is believing that there can be more to life, that a horizon beyond death exists, is not this wishful thinking, metaphysical speculation, a pathetic self-misunderstanding? Is there really any way of living with hope that is not self-deceived?

For his own part, Paul characterizes the difference between the way of hope, on the one hand, and the way of despair, on the other, as turning on the choice of whether to pursue spiritual drink or to instead settle for earthly drink, respectively. The juxtaposition is one implying the authentic conceivability of a mode of life unknown to the carnal man. This is no small result. For even if somebody is resistant to conceding that there could be more to existence than mere earthly things, it nevertheless is impossible to with certainty rule out such a possibility. But if there is room for possibility, so too then hope.

Such a hypothesis (if one may be forgiven for putting it in those terms) is elucidated in John's Gospel, where it serves as the occasion for an illuminating exchange between Jesus Christ and the Samaritan woman at the well. In discussing the possibility of this previously unimaginable way of life, this way of hope, this way of the spirit, their talk turns to the subject of the living waters said to characterize it. These are waters that Christ alone, and no earthly drink, can give. We read about this donation elsewhere, when in Paul's same remarks to the Corinthians regarding the prophets, he says, "And did all drink the same spiritual drink: for they drank of that spiritual Rock that followed them: and that Rock was Christ" (1 Cor. 10:4). That nobody except Christ can quench this thirst—the thirst for meaning, for hope, for peace, for joy—is a necessity. Predictably, it accordingly was a topic of prophecy. If on the occasion recorded in the Acts in which Paul was able to convince the crowds of his gospel through "showing by the scriptures that Jesus was Christ" (Acts 18:28), Paul's demonstration proved possible in virtue of Christ's having already shown two of his disciples how the prophets had foretold of him in the scriptures. Two disciples on the road to Emmaus meet a stranger whom they do not recognize to be the Risen One. On the journey, he mentions the scriptures that tell them all "the things concerning himself" (Luke 24:27). Luke's account does not specify which particular scriptures Christ discussed with the disciples. But we may make informed conjectures. If the prophets themselves drank of the Spirit, as Paul says to the Corinthians they did, were these not the same spiritual waters for which King David also yearned? We read so: "And David longed, and said, Oh that one would give me drink of the water of the well of Bethlehem, that is at the gate!" (1 Chron. 11:17). David's thirst intimates the desire for the living waters that Christ will bestow, the waters that Christ speaks of to the Samaritan woman at the well. For if it is only the well at Bethlehem that can satisfy David's thirst, it is because his thirst anticipates the incarnation later to occur there in Bethlehem. Further light is shed on the nature of David's spiritual longing when we are told more about it at the conclusion of the exchange between Christ at the well. For in response to the woman's stating that she desires to receive this spiritual water capable of quenching her thirst, Christ says of these waters that they give without ceasing, waters of life, waters that give the rest no earthly waters do: "Whosoever drinketh of this water shall thirst again. But whosoever drinketh of the water that I shall give him shall never thirst: but the water that I shall give him shall be in him a water springing up into everlasting life" (John 4:13–14). These are waters that quench the thirst for meaning, infinite waters that slake the spirit, unlike the carnal desire for finite things that leaves us thirsty. The mere mention of these waters invites a question. If there are such waters, and if they alone are said to be capable of quenching this thirst that no others are, why do so many who thirst nevertheless reject these waters? Why do they choose to remain thirsty? Why not only refuse to drink the living water, but deny its very existence?

To answer, it is necessary to revisit the connection between drunkenness and sleep. To taste the waters—the waters of Life—one must first awake from the sleep forbidding access to them. To drink of them will require waking from sleep to meet the day, to no longer be drunken, but to be sober-minded. In short, drinking the waters of life will consist in entering a faith whose very form of lucidity drunkenness had clouded. It is with these spiritual stakes in view that Paul's words of admonition against drunkenness to the Corinthians are to be understood. If, as he says, drunkards will not inherit the kingdom of Heaven (1 Cor. 6:9), is not this precisely because drunkenness signals faithlessness? Bearing in mind this equivalence between them, the drunkard's weariness is seen to be rooted in the spiritlessness unfurling it. To go *this* way, to choose the cup of drunkenness, to choose hedonism and materialism, is to choose death. Even those who carnally speaking do not drink and thus are sober, are consequently without faith, for, in the relevant spiritual respect, they are still intoxicated. They may not fill the time with spirits and liquors, but their own preoccupations, whatever they may be, are earthly. From this perspective, there is an equivalence between the faithless who drink to drunkenness, on the one hand, and those who entirely abstain yet remain without faith, on the other. Indeed, considered spiritually, it might even be the drunkards, who, in not inhibiting the true depths of their despair are closer to spiritual recovery than those, who, complacent in their insensibility, find no need to drown the sorrows of a hopeless heart.

By way of considering the symbolic status of drunkenness, have we not arrived upon the borderlands of life's most momentous decision? No doubt we have. For, here, we are faced with the choice between faith and disbelief, the choice earlier confronting Ostade's three drunkards in the tavern. It is easy to find additional biblical examples in which drunkenness is associated with sleep, and whereby the latter is taken to be a figure of faithlessness. We shall restrict our attention to one. The case at hand is described in the eleventh chapter of Matthew's Gospel. Having begun his ministry to the cities, Christ addresses those who are denying he is the Son of God.

To reply, he chooses the lens of drunkenness to explain himself. When it came to John the Baptist, as he reminds his listeners, John's righteousness was made manifest by his sobriety. And yet, the Pharisees discounted it: "For John came neither eating nor drinking, and they say, He hath a devil" (Matt. 11:18). Just as the angel of the Lord had told Zacharias would be so, the prophecy concerning his son John was fulfilled: "he shall be great in the sight of the Lord, and shall drink neither wine nor strong drink; and he shall be filled with the Holy Ghost, even from his mother's womb" (Luke 1:15). However, John's sobriety is insufficient to convince the eyes of doubt that he indeed is the one he says. As Matthew's narrative goes on to observe, the fact that some accuse John of unrighteousness despite his sobriety means that, if such sobriety is insufficient for establishing one's genuine claim to righteousness, it is because drunkenness itself happens to involve more than natural intoxication, but spiritual offense. We appreciate so for ourselves when we read later in that same stretch of text how drinking can be used as a convenient excuse by the unbelieving to question someone's righteousness. This way of questioning somebody's righteousness is one the Pharisees use against Jesus: "The Son of man came eating and drinking, and they say, Behold a man gluttonous, and a winebibber, a friend of publicans and sinners" (Matt. 11:19). This is the hypocrisy of doubt. For no matter what it sees, it will find a way to interpret what it sees as evidence against the truth of what it does not want to see. In one case, doubt dismisses what in fact is immediately evident, while in the other, it refuses to see beyond the superficial appearance. In this first case with John, doubt denies the obvious; in the other with Christ, it insists upon a semblance of obviousness, without ever considering further into what it knows would thereby contradict the initial impression. Hence, because it wants to believe John is an imposter (that he is not a prophet), it ignores his obvious righteousness. And, because it wants to believe that Jesus is not the Christ, so accordingly it saddles him with an only apparent, yet ultimately misleading, unrighteousness. Doubt, then, comes in two forms of blindness: with John, an unduly suspicious seeing that does not see what meets the eye, simply because it does not want to see it; with Christ, a self-servingly shallow seeing that sees only enough to be able to remain blind to whatever more it does not want to see.

What here concerns us, however, is not so much the origin of the false rumors circulating about John and Christ, or the significance of the company they kept, but rather the underlying fact that their words and deeds put drunkenness in a spiritual frame. Drunkenness is a matter of sleep precisely in that it first of all is one of unfaith. This is the lesson of the texts under consideration. For if some such as John the Baptist are falsely accused of unrighteousness despite their sobriety, while others like Christ are accused of unrighteousness for merely having associated with those who drink, then these baseless judgments miss their mark, not only because they are false, but because they fail to see the spiritual significance of the entire matter. They miss the depths at stake. Not seeing that the issue above all is one of faith, they are blind. The preceding episode in Matthew, for instance, reveals that righteousness, when understood in its spiritual dimension, is not a matter of whether or not one drinks alcohol. The reason, as we have seen, is that drunkenness itself symbolizes more than the mere state of natural intoxication. It is a spiritual intoxication, the condition of unbelief, which is capable of afflicting the teetotaler as much as it does the winebibber. Transposed from a territory defined in terms of the opposition between sobriety and carnal intoxication, drunkenness is reassigned to another, and deeper, spiritual register. Ultimately, what establishes John the Baptist's and Christ's righteousness is not their alcohol habits, but the fact that each drinks of the same Spirit, the drink which the unbelieving do not drink.

More essentially than natural intoxication, drunkenness is a supernatural stupor. It is in this sense, that the drunkard is said to sleep. In turn, nothing of fundamental consequence separates sober unbelief from Bacchanalian revelry. Both sleep the same sleep of faithlessness. True sobriety becomes a metaphor for salvation, since to be sober is to be awake, which is to say, not to be drunk, but to have faith—to be awake through having drunk the spiritual drink of Christ.

"Nothing," Tertullian says in *On the Resurrection of the Flesh*, "perishes but with a view to salvation."[5] The seasons pass away to return again, day turns to night, and night back to day. These "parables of nature" reveal how everything about creation is infused by the "instinct [for] renewal."[6] Each and every day, the possibility of awaking from sleep always resides with us. It is with faith's wakefulness in view that Christ instructs those who have heard him not to again fall asleep, having waked from the slumber of the old days of unbelief, but to stay awake and keep watch, and, lighting the lamp of the soul, to keep vigil: "And what I say unto you I say unto all, Watch" (Mark 13:37). The task of keeping watch falls to each of us. For in that peculiar stillness amid the dark blues of moonlit walls, one lies alone, and, drifting off to sleep, either heeds or not God's call to "remember thee upon one's bed, and meditate on thee in the night watches" (Psalm 63:6). There, in moments as these, encompassed by the room's night solitude, eternity looms. And so, the day concludes in decision. Will one prefer the restlessness of sleep, or the great awakening of faith?

Chapter 2

The Strong Wind and a Still Small Voice

If sometimes we sleep spiritually, living unappreciatively of all the good that has been given to us, unconcerned with the higher tasks that we are being called to embark upon but have deferred, inured to the dangers our present course of either complacency or defiance is currently leading us, what about God? Does God, like us, sleep?

The suggestion, quite rightly, is one likely to strike us as absurd on its face. Potential Christological complications aside, God, who is in some genuine sense all-knowing, is aware of everything, not least of all us, and our present standing toward him. As consoling a truth as this can be, accepting it is not a foregone conclusion. It takes effort and attention. Here, to be sure, is a truth that must be internalized, one permanently calling upon our resolve to live by. It is one expecting and requiring a commitment of us, not something simply to be beheld idly or understood emptily. At stake, in short, is more than a proposition to entertain, for God is aiming to initiate us into a form of existence whose first distinguishable feature is our having submitted to it, and no matter the cost. Henceforth, the resulting life assumes the form of a trial. And if it is a trial, it is so because, leaving behind the old way of making decisions only with an eye to what falls under the purview of our personal foresight, and now instead stretching ourselves into the great beyond of the unknowable, above all, it will test our trust.

Such is the lesson life's circumstances teach Elijah, as the events concerned are recounted in 1 Kings. Turning to the scene, we find him asleep under a juniper tree. As Juan Antonio Frias y Escalante's *An Angel Awakens the Prophet Elijah* (1667) shows, this is somebody who is not only tired, but in need. But of what?

Certainly, Elijah's strain is bodily. He is thirsty and hungry. He is exhausted, his strength drained by the desert heat. So, he has crumpled into a despondent sleep to escape the fatigue. The brush, however, provides little comfort; the shade is scant, and it would not provide much of a refuge anyhow, even if it were lusher than it is, given the situation being what it is. For what is really testing the thresholds of Elijah's endurance is not so much the natural, immediate needs for food and drink or rest. Although the jug placed prominently at his left hand by the consoling angel attests to his thirst, it also indicates why Elijah finds himself thirsty, why, that is to say, he has willingly plunged himself into such a dire position to begin with. The precariousness of his circumstances imbues the jug with a symbolic significance, the jug representing the need for spiritual sustenance—for a nourishing strength only God is able to give. As we see, Elijah's journey into the desert is forcing him to near the limits of the bearable, an intolerable situation almost, not due simply to the harsh conditions he is meeting there, but, more deeply, to what he is fleeing, to a condition from which he wants to escape but cannot outrun. For, the farther he attempts to flee from what threatens him from behind, the clearer the situation's unsurpassable danger becomes. In fleeing to the wilderness, it only becomes clearer that Elijah, burdened heavily by concerns and fears, is above all burdened by a self-imposed weight, the weight of his own misperceptions. Are not we sometimes our own worst enemy, the true cause of our own despondence?

This will be the insight Elijah comes to slowly. As the text recounts, Jezebel, the wife of King Ahab, has vowed to kill Elijah in retribution for what he has just done to flout her authority, having successfully challenged her prophets of Baal in a contest testing the mettle of their god and Elijah's own Yahweh, the Lord God of Israel. As the people discover, Elijah serves the more powerful and faithful divinity, the true and living divinity, in short. Consequently, in the immediate aftermath of this humiliating public setback regarding her efforts to keep the hearts of Israel loyal to Baal, one beginning with her prophets' sacrificial offering never catching flame, and then concluding with their being slain by sword, Jezebel is livid, and out for blood: "Then Jezebel sent a messenger unto Elijah, saying, So let the gods do *to me*, and more also, if I make not thy life as the life of one of them by tomorrow about this time" (1 Kings 19:2). Convinced his plight is irrevocable, the danger too overwhelming, the cause unsalvageable, he a day's journey into the wilderness despairingly asks God to "take away [his] life" (1 Kings 19:4) before drifting asleep.

While it begins in weakness, Elijah's ultimately is the sleep that strengthens. In Escalante's rendering of the moments before waking up, the prophet lies asleep with his head on a stone, chin to his chest, face pointing toward us, with his back turned to an angel, who, standing right over him, has laid his left hand gently on Elijah's shoulder, the angel's other hand's extended forefinger still reaching to touch the sleeper's cheek. About to be stirred from sleep, Elijah will find that he is no longer alone, or better, that he never had been alone. God is with him, though he may have lost sight of the fact. The water he has been given to drink is a reminder of his dependence on God. The Almighty's hand does not just give us things. It beckons us to draw nearer to him.

This spiritual dependence is the subject of Ferdinand Bol's *Elijah Fed by an Angel* (c. 1660–63). Bol, who studied under Rembrandt, and who completed the piece around the time of his first wife's death, affirms the human need to believe there always is room for hope, even and especially in our worst hours of trouble. Bol shows the angel approaching Elijah from the sleeper's side, the angel laying a hand on the prophet's near shoulder. Unlike Escalante's portrayal which placed Elijah still in the act of sleeping, Bol shows him already awake, Elijah now looking up, his back leaning against the juniper tree's trunk, his legs splayed out rather comfortably. A clear, warm golden-hued atmosphere of relief has settled down over things. His left arm, cocked at the elbow, lifts upward, as if he is still mentally discombobulated by the shock of being suddenly awoken. Not only does he find himself awake unexpectedly, but at the foot of an angel! And yet, he is not without some orientation. His right arm, seemingly possessed of a mind of its own, is already groping for the morsel of bread laying at his feet below the jug of water at his knee. He looks directly at the angel, but the angel, whose hand has been outstretched to the weary prophet, is intent on doing more than only waking him from his slumber. This angel is not here to console only. There is a trace of gentle, but firm, reproach in the helping hand's gesture, as if the angel, resting his hand on Elijah's shoulder, is thereby reminding his human counterpart not to reach for the bread without first stopping to grasp the deeper significance of the circumstances. Yes, bread and water are available for Elijah's nourishment. But he must not be so shortsighted, must not overlook the magnitude of their offering. Bol's angel, in brief, comports himself in a way reminding us that Elijah is being fed bread, yes, but more than bread.

A loaf of bread and a jug of water meet Elijah's needs, as the angel knows. He comes bearing them for that reason. The bread he offers in Elijah's moment of hunger comes with a challenge, though. To accept it gratefully, as it deserves to be had, as the gift it is, Elijah must awaken to the situation's higher stakes. Taking things for granted can become routine when we forget that we are not the originators of what we possess. Even the most basic of externalities that we enjoy, such as food and water, are provided to us. And richer things like companionship and community, things that make our life distinctively human, depend on structures that must already be in place. These "sovereign expressions of life" as K.E. Løgstrup insightfully called them, the openness of speech, mercy, hope, trust, and love, allow us to function and flourish, for without them none of our everyday pursuits, however mundane, would be possible. None of us has brought these states of affairs into being. Rather, we find things already intelligibly arranged so as to support and promote our activities and pursuits. To forget this, to plunge headlong into life's busyness insensitive to the ordinances of life that have made doing so possible, is prideful. Leading us to act as if we are the ground of everything, this is an egocentrism that accordingly blinds.

During his travels, Elijah is always in danger of slipping into this forgetfulness, this illusion of false independence. The wilderness encounter with the angel, so he must realize, is God's attempt to stir him to see the spiritual trial in which he has been placed, one calling for a renewed humility, and, in turn, a fuller trust in God than what he theretofore has shown. Everyone needs bread and water. But how much more so the word of God, the angel coming to Elijah's rescue counsels! What in Escalante's painting had appeared at first to be a physical sleep, a sleep of purely bodily exhaustion, is here shown by Bol to be a pivotal moment whereby Elijah, having been awakened to his forgetfulness of God, can both identify and correct his failings, and come to appreciate the full depths of his dependence. By fulfilling the basic needs of hunger and thirst that Elijah owing to circumstances can no longer fulfill for himself, the angel, presumably without saying a word about it, reminds him that without God the adversity in the wilderness is sure to vanquish him. Elijah receives an unequivocal lesson in human life's fragility and dependence, and so in turn a reminder of the mistake of forgetting these ordinances of life that Løgstrup observes make life livable. The Apocrypha states the lesson plainly: "The beginning of pride is when one departeth from God, and his heart is turned away from his Maker" (Ecclus. 10:12).

It is one thing to forget God altogether, losing sight of our powerlessness to provide for ourselves without him, but there are still more subtle forms such pride can further take. There is, for example, the ever fluid boundary between a bold confidence in God, on the one hand, and a prideful self-confidence, on the other. Elijah is somebody who inspires others with his righteousness born of confidence in God. On closer inspection, though, this righteous figure whom the woman of Zarephath had said to be a "man of God" and in whom "the word of the Lord in his mouth was truth" (1 Kings 17:24), is himself always hanging at the precipice of forgetting that divine word, and so consequently in danger of falling into hypocrisy. For as Elijah's journey attests, oftentimes forgetting God takes the form of not living up to the very words of wisdom we offer others. We see their failings, and what they can do to correct them. We see their weaknesses, and what they should do to improve. We see their mistakes, and what they can do to avoid committing them again. It can all seem so easy, because it is all so obvious. When the text initially introduces us to Elijah, it is with his prophesizing to Ahab a prolonged period of no rain as punishment for the king's and his people's unfaithfulness to God: "As the Lord God of Israel liveth, before whom I stand, there shall not be dew nor rain these years, but according to my word" (1 Kings 17:1). After the confrontation with Ahab, the next verse relates that the "word of the Lord" instructs Elijah to head toward the Jordan, whereupon he is fed by the ravens at the brook. When, thus, he is in turn told by God to travel onward to the village of Zarephath, it is a bit surprising that, even despite knowing there is to be no rain to come for some time, and even despite having already experienced his needs having been provided for at God's hand by the ravens, Elijah has such little patience for the townswoman he encounters there. He asks her to bring him food, but the woman, worried for her wellbeing and that of her son in light of a looming food shortage, is reluctant to give away the last of it. In reply, without hesitation, he exhorts her, quite correctly, to trust God and so to take heart: "Fear not [...] For thus saith the Lord God of Israel, The barrel of meal shall not waste, neither shall the cruse of oil fail, until the day that the Lord sendeth rain upon the earth" (1 Kings 17:13–14). And when shortly afterward Elijah raises the widow's son from the dead (1 Kings 17:17–24), it is because, and only because, God in compassion hears the voice of his plea. And once again, when Elijah after this leg of the sojourn returns to confront Ahab, the advice he offers to the fearful Obadiah—God is with them, and thus there is nothing to fear of Baal's prophets and Ahab—is sound counsel.

So by the time the angel of the Lord comes to Elijah's own aid in the wilderness, it accordingly is not to bear food and water only, but also a needed message. Previously, if Elijah was in a position to tell others how they should face their own daunting situations, reminding them as he does of their dependence on God and hence the corresponding importance of trusting God, it was only to the extent that Elijah, listening to the voice of God, and going where he was told to go, was situated to offer such counsel. His movements were not happenstance wanderings. They were destinations firmly set by God. It makes sense to heed the spiritual advice of somebody who encounters us along his own journey set out by trusting God. It makes far less sense, however, to listen to somebody telling us to trust God who himself does not. Fleeing Jezebel by instinct and fear, rather than at the direction of God, Elijah temporarily abandons his journey, jeopardizing his spiritual credibility. He has failed to trust God in the way he has been telling others to trust.

When the angel visits Elijah abandoned in the wilderness without either water or food, it is to deliver a wakeup call, and in two ways. The angel, first, gets Elijah to rise from sleep, but also reminds the disconsolate prophet of his own responsibility for his current plight. If Elijah is to reclaim the clarity of purpose that once had inspired others, he must renew his own trust in God, an entire reorientation demanding he come again to view his life as a journey overseen by God. To regain his proper footing, in short, he needs to rediscover the right path, the one that opens to us only through listening to the voice of God, rather than seeking the immediate path laid out by what seems best in our own sight: "Trust in the Lord with all thine heart; and lean not unto thine own understanding. In all thy ways acknowledge him, and he shall direct thy paths" (Prov 3:5–6). When we choose our own way, we enjoy the false comfort of thinking that because we have set our own goal or destination, we are thereby in control, masters over ourselves and everything that may befall us. There is a feeling of security in it, that we have assurance in setting out to accomplish what we have determined for ourselves to be worthy of our time and our effort. This is the seductive illusion of autonomy, that a life determined by what we alone are willing to pursue is somehow safe and satisfying. If it is too easy to settle for this life of apparent security and ease, it is because it is rooted, however subtly, in the pride of refusing to seek a strength beyond our own. In a theme that comes increasingly into view in following Elijah more carefully, we see that, rather than seeking the joy of the Lord which opens us to an unforeseen and incalculable future, the self-satisfied life seeks instead enjoyment in itself and its own power of foresight. Hence, finding the right path will first require humility, a recognition that what is truly worth pursuing entails our depending on God, and not ourselves alone, in order to achieve what it is that must be accomplished. Otherwise, even the goal we are successful in achieving is only a failure, for, even in accomplishing it, we have failed to set the goal God would have set for us, and instead pursued a poor substitute of our own choosing. By contrast, accomplishing the success that we are called to by God requires us to envision triumph in a situation which, considered by own our lights, would seem to portend certain failure. It means contending with what for us alone is impossible. As the angel informs Elijah, he will be too frail to finish on his own the journey God has appointed him: "And the angel of the Lord came again the second time, and touched him, and said, Arise and eat; because the journey is too great for thee" (1 Kings 19:7). Finding the true path means accepting that we must abandon the false sense of independence that tells us to cling to ourselves, as if our security depended on keeping God from interfering in our affairs. Only then can we overcome our limits.

The fact that Elijah in this regard had himself lost his way despite having been instructing others of how to find theirs, is highlighted beautifully by Francesco Maggiotto's *The Feeding of Elijah by the Angel* (1780). Maggiotto's painting does not present the physically exhausted sleeping figure of Escalante or the shocked one of Bol, but rather an Elijah ready to answer the angel's gift offerings, not with gratitude or enjoyment, but with griping. Lounging on some steps, his left elbow resting on the slab above him, his head on his chin, right arm raised widely in a gesture of impatience, it is as if he is wondering what has taken the angel so long to arrive to his rescue. This is a disgruntled servant, somebody with the attitude that he has been asked to do too much, and somebody convinced of the justifiability of his irritation with his predicament. This is neither the exhausted, despairing Elijah, nor the shocked and grateful Elijah, but an entitled one. Just as the jug and bread lie out of reach in the left corner of the painting's foreground, so too the angel's outstretched arm hovering over Elijah's shoulder appears to gesture him to just stand up and carry on. Whereas in other works in the genre the angel has wings, but is nevertheless on foot, firmly on the ground, sensitive to Elijah's earthly and frail frame, here instead the angel is suspended in the air, whisking over him, as if to maintain the authority by preserving the celestial distance between them, and refusing to indulge Elijah's moans and complaints. Maggiotto's rendering has noticed, and exploited, a feature of the biblical account: Elijah, who had so much to say to others, would have done well to heed his own advice about trusting God. After all, had he done so, he wouldn't be in need of rescue from a crisis of his own making. All the better, then, so the angel seems to communicate, to not indulge Elijah's bad attitude, but to try to correct him and to set him back on the right path.

That Elijah's restoration requires an admission of his own dependence on God, a dependence which will demand a recognition of his failure to have trusted God when he fled from Jezebel, Alessandro Bonvicino Moretto's *Elijah Visited by an Angel* (1534) captures so well. In this Renaissance altar piece, Elijah is depicted in anguish, his face contorted by the torment of his fatigue. Unlike with the Maggiotto, we see that the source of the pain is rooted in a realistic appraisal of the arduous journey still left to complete, and not simply any personal failings or mistakes of stubbornness or pride that have led him to find himself here. Collapsed with his side resting on a half-wall, eyes closed, palm up against his head, Elijah's hand clutches the wall. The angel standing behind him rests a hand on his head. The sight of a castle off in the far background—possibly Mount Horeb—is a reminder of the long, windy road lying ahead for this servant of God. Yet here, the food and water are close to hand, a positive indication that Elijah's burden perhaps is not so bleak as he felt it to be before the angel's welcome arrival. In any case, the pride and ingratitude of Maggiotto's rendering is absent. This is an Elijah who, however tired and anguished he may be, accepts it is possible to go on in knowledge that God is there to assist him. If he has brought peril on himself, he is contrite about it. And if he felt before like he had nowhere to go but to die alone in the wilderness, now he sees a future, and a way forward.

Even if God's ways are mysterious, it is fair to ask: why, of all places, to Mount Horeb? God foreshadows his reasoning for having sent Elijah there when the latter reaches the mountain, and is told to await word: "Go outside and stand on the mountain before the Lord" (1 Kings 19:11). Elijah does so, and in a moment, "a great strong wind rent the mountains, and brake in pieces the rocks before the Lord;" and "after the wind an earthquake," and "then a fire" (1 Kings 19:11–12). And yet, the Lord is not in the strong wind, or the earthquake, or the fire. The voice of God is heard speaking to him, at last, only "in a still small voice." When afterward God questions Elijah as to why the latter thinks he has been brought to Mount Horeb, Elijah still cannot entirely banish the nagging idea that he has been left to oppose Baal and his prophets, a lone survivor who is isolated and unappreciated. But he is wrong! As it happens, he is far from alone. As God reveals, "Yet I have left me seven thousand in Israel, all the knees which have not bowed unto Baal, and every mouth which hath not kissed him" (1 Kings 19:18). Experience will teach us in time not to look to others for validation or approval, but to look to God. One reason for this is that when others are disappointing us, or seem to be, it can lead to bitterness if we dwell on it. Our frustration with others over time corrodes our will, and may lead us to giving up, to leaving unfinished the work that God has appointed us to undertake. And so, this is the uplifting, but humbling, lesson Elijah learns. For contrary to the original assumption responsible for his despondence, he is not alone. In fact, there exist seven thousand others just like him, those who have also remained faithful by not worshipping Baal. Elijah had not known so, and if he had treated what from his perspective appeared to be the case as if it were the case, he likely would have quit. Shown the meagerness of his knowledge, Elijah experiences what Paul, writing in his letter to the Ephesians, later states explicitly, that God "is able to do exceeding abundantly above all that we ask or think" (Eph. 3:20). It is not such a rare thing for events to reveal to us how little we had known. As for providence, are not God and his plans for us much bigger than what we can conceive? Understanding the immensity of God, and the extent to which his plans for us defy what our own limited perspective might suggest, is not only a profound source of joy, but even perhaps the very essence of it. Joy is unshakeable, for it is unconditional. If we sometimes feel alone, misunderstood or unappreciated, engaged in a struggle against all odds, we must recognize that what we experience is partial at best. God has the full picture, while we do not. And if we accept that our perspective is just that—a perspective—then for all we know, there are others out there who feel just as alone as us. What matters is that each of us looks to God for strength. As Elijah learns, everything good, including the comforts of true safety and security, never depends on our whereabouts or other circumstances, but on our attitude, an attitude acceding to the reality that here, before God, we can find refuge always: "God is our refuge and strength, a very present help in trouble. Therefore will not we fear, though the earth be removed, and though the mountains be carried into the midst of the sea; Though the waters thereof roar and be troubled, though the mountains shake with the swelling thereof" (Psalm 46:1–3). Refuge, so we see along with Elijah, is neither to be found among others, nor alone in the wilderness, nor in the cave. Safety cannot be secured by belonging to a crowd, or by living alone in self-sufficient isolation. It is found through the hope in God.

This hope is a feature of the joy of the Lord. Something of the awe and reverence owed to God's providence is captured in Paul Gustave Doré's engraving Prophet Elijah Fed by an Angel (1866). In 1843, the Vulgate appeared in French. Shortly thereafter, Doré and fellow laborers in 1866 published La Grande Bible de Tours, an illustrated book of hundreds of engravings depicting events from both the Old and New Testaments. Still relatively young at the time (Doré was born in Strasbourg on January 6, 1832), he was by then already renowned with the Parisian public for his work on Dante, among other things. And while much of his work is distinctive for its spectacular style naturally tailored to the cataclysmic death and destruction recounted in the Old Testament, here the artist's delicate touch for mercy is put on display in his vision of Elijah's deliverance. It is no small wonder the work emphasizes both awe and peace equally at once, since, as anyone who views the work will gather that Doré must have himself understood well, one of the underlying, edifying takeaways regarding the sequence of events told of Elijah in the Bible is God's unflagging faithfulness throughout. Elijah learns, as Doré shows, that God never abandons those who place their trust in him. No doubt with an eye to Elijah and others like him, for this reason the Apostle Peter can say, "For the eyes of the Lord are over the righteous, and his ears are open unto their prayers" (1 Pet. 3:12).

We are returned to the issue of dependence and need, of satisfaction and fulfillment. "Blessed are those who thirst and hunger for righteousness for they shall be filled" (Matt. 5:6), says Christ in the Sermon on the Mount. Bread and water— two things absolutely essential to Elijah's journey, yet still not nearly as imperative as the word of God. Christ's teaching is overwhelming, in part, no doubt, for how subversive of our everyday attitude it is, as anyone who fasts for a day and then considers, while still hungry, what it means for the word of God to be more important than bread! For Elijah, what inspires him, drives him, sustains him, fulfills him—in short, what renders him capable of achieving what would otherwise be beyond his limits, is this ideal of a hungry existence, of living by every word of God. Maggiatto's scene of Elijah's visit from the angel captured the figure of the one who lives without grace, who, trying to do it alone, falls into resentment, and eventually, despair. Whoever accepts God's hand, by contrast, no longer walks alone, but takes wings like the angel. As Elijah's fellow prophet Isaiah says, such is the one who perseveres through the strength of God: "He giveth power to the faint; and to them that have no might he increaseth strength. Even the youths shall faint and be weary, and the young men shall utterly fall: But they that wait upon the LORD shall renew their strength; they shall mount up with wings as eagles; they shall run, and not be weary; and they shall walk, and not faint" (Isa. 40:29–31). If, then, all of these exquisite paintings of Elijah's journey suggest more than a hint of a Christophany in the events they depict so admirably, is it not because pondering them turns us not only to the prophet, but also invariably to ourselves, to how our own trials bear a likeness to his? Unmistakably, there is something universal at work in these trials, something transcending the geographical and historical particularities of the biblical account. The lessons they teach are fitting, because they underscore the everyday ordinances of life that have been laid down by God: courage in the face of evil, hope in adversity, equanimity in the face of sufferings, humility to accept our limitations, trust in what lies beyond us. These are the characteristics of the kenotic existence made possible for us when we hear the word of God. And these lessons that form Elijah on his way can form us on ours. Elijah's strength was the joy of the Lord, and his hope was in the Lord. It does not take a journey to a faraway place, to realize the same should be true for us. All that is necessary is a searching attention into whatever place is now ours. Always with us, God's voice can never be wholly forgotten or ignored. Only at our own peril do we try.

Chapter 3

On the Broad Way

In a way, everything we come to regret about ourselves in life, and here our past evils are certainly no exception but often these moments of piercing rumination's sharpest instance, derives from the desire, at once as insatiable as it is misdirected, to find peace by possessing what we fear to lose, of what we fear to live without. We cling to dreams of recovering what is gone, or continue to struggle toward some illusory future of what will never be, in either case content to fester over our self-induced burdens that we wear in like an old pair of shoes. Just as Henry David Thoreau observed correctly, this is the life of quiet desperation that in fact partly enjoys itself. It is a life of the failed desire born of our fears, above all, the fear to change. The fear of God, by contrast, is otherwise, unfurling as it does according to a wholly different regime of desire, lest it fail to be the beginning of wisdom that everyone who comes to find it pleasantly discovers it is. If it were not so, if the fear of God were like other fears, an item of obsession or concern forever ejecting us onto a frenzied hunt for that which has disturbed us, and so what in turn would continually resist our attempts to tame, then it would procure only more of the same haunting absence to which the desire for possession's vain quest for satisfaction ends. But it is not so, for the way beginning with the fear of God leads to contentment, and ultimately because it is not at all possessive. For rather than seek the self-possession this first desire, this desire unto regret, thinks can be secured by possessing whatever it mistakes itself to need, true desire relents, and so finally lets go, finding itself mercifully at last secure in the complete self-abandonment that leads to God. In trying to possess ourselves through possessing what we do not yet possess (or fear to live without possessing), unintentionally we lose ourselves, and without noticing. Only instead by first choosing to lose ourselves, not through the doomed expedition to find ourselves in possessions, but rather through abandoning that very desire to so possess, do we find what we sought but could not find previously, the true security that comes from God but never things, the salvation infinitely higher and securer than anything we could have attained through the desire that had been obstructing and diverting that divine need. And so, it is with these contrasting ends of desire in view that Christ says what he does, reiterating plainly what we always already knew desire itself to have been telling us, even when we were disregarding it, and so therefore were lost: "For whoever desires to save his life will lose it, but whoever loses his life for My sake will save it" (Luke 9:24). That what we really need is God, not what our unchecked fears lead us to desire, is a lesson we come to understand only once we accept that we ought not to fear anything except desire's very power to lead us astray through fear, if we are not careful. Desire's transfiguration, from inattentive or feverish, on the one hand, to attentive and judicious, on the other, is an upheaval of everything, that great moment of lucidity marking the fear of God, the beginning of wisdom when desire has learned what fear is, and so accordingly what is worth fearing. Here, in God, passing through a fear of the wasteland that we have reached by way of desires now to be regretted, we break free, and, unfettered, at last find ourselves.

Consequently, there are two ways, and precisely two ways, to desire, the first one that is lost, blinded and consumed by the anguish of its fearful distresses and vain yearnings, and then the other, the one way that has found freedom in having unencumbered itself of its old delusions, finding itself now fulfilled in good choices and habits, this new life that delights itself in the joy of God wisdom brings.

Regardless of how acutely life's profane troubles consume

us, they do not warrant the title of tribulations. The ending of a tumultuous love affair, the compulsive worry over whether one will receive the job promotion, a struggle for prestige against a rival at the annual neighborhood holiday party, though such episodes certainly matter to those involved, they are not genuine crucibles. True tribulation tests us in a way always holding out the possibility, however slight, of success. There exists the possibility for profound improvement, of a self-transformation for the better. But to be consumed by the troubles associated with possession's desire has no such hope of success, for it is to be sucked into a bottomless vortex, a ceaseless swirl of worries and concerns weighing us down, and, eventually, crushing us beneath the weight of that burden. To undergo the whirlwinds of this desire seeking peace in something besides God, hence, is to lose oneself — to lose oneself in the sense that one can be said to serve a lost cause, as, for instance, the losing military commander who, resigned to his fate, grimly orders his depleted forces to counterattack in a furious yet futile last stand, in short, to lose oneself in such a way as to surely find only disappointment where there can be no hope of any lasting satisfaction. Inevitably, this desire devours us.

Auguste Rodin's foreboding statue *The Three Shades* (1886) puts this desire's hopelessness squarely on view. Here before us stand three figures set on destruction. Originally produced for his awesome *The Gates of Hell* imagining of Dante's *Inferno*, the statue's shades protrude toward and descend upon us, bringing to mind the famous dread-inducing inscription associated with the literary scene it conjures: "Abandon every hope, who enter here." In encountering Rodin's work, suddenly our place is no longer amid the cheerful, bustling throngs of the Musée d'Orsay, but elsewhere, for we are transported to a place of solitary contemplation. In the presence of the complete piece, looking up, our eyes inevitably turn to the sitting *Thinker* atop the gates. One wonders. Is it Rodin himself broodingly meditating over his work? Or, rather, is it actually us, we who are now placed in the presence of a sight impelling us to consider the current condition of our soul? Not light viewing, to be sure! Probably, this is why so many of the museum visitors pass swiftly by, and do not stop to look at what would bring them to a halt, interrupting them, forcing them to think, to wrestle with all of life's heavy questions from which everything else around us conspires to distract us. If a common theory has interpreted the thinker as neither Dante considering his characters nor Rodin beholding his composition, but rather the first man himself, Adam, viewing the consequences of his sin, would it not then be more accurate to say that the thinking figure is us, the one who now stands before himself?

While Rodin in Paris was wrestling with eternity in the Hôtel Biron, the Norwegian painter and printmaker Edvard Munch was in Oslo doing so too, exploring the modulations of our inner being in all its variety, though, to be sure, almost always with a focus on the macabre and melancholic. The result of his efforts are engrossing studies in contorted desire, of anxious desire leading to dissolution and disconsolateness. Munch's *The Scream* (1893) is far and away the most famous work of the type from him, of an artwork that channels its artist's own torment, but there are many other examples from his early period as well. At the heart of Munch's prolific output—thousands of paintings, woodcuts, etchings, lithographs, photographs and other paraphernalia were found in his house upon his death in 1944—is the creativity fueled by anxiety, an anxiety that for him, as with most who flirt with it, became a dependency, a muse without which the painter could not envision himself being able to create. Dark anxiety, which sucked him under like an undertow, down to the very bottoms of anguish, morphed into a stimulant, a spiritual amphetamine whose intoxicating powers distorted everything that he saw in a way thereby rendering it worthy of expression. Munch once said, "Without anxiety and illness, I am a ship without a rudder [....] My sufferings are part of my self and my art. They are indistinguishable from me, and their destruction would destroy my art." Here, there is no mistaking, is an eye that has come to see beauty only by way of pain, a look infatuated with its own sadness, one no longer trusting that things, if left to themselves, are able to reward the one who beholds their presence. And so, this look drapes things in its sadness, storing them in its mausoleum of sorrow. Such despair desires to take solace in itself, enjoys the project of nourishing this sadness that feels a triumphant nobility in its isolated, gentle aloofness.

It would be dishonest to deny this attitude and what it is capable of seeing their element of beauty. Nevertheless, at the same time, this appreciation for beauty, the beauty of sadness, delicate and poignant though it may be, detaches itself dangerously from anything but the play of emotions. Accordingly, it comes to find even its resulting creativity to be a prison. Woe is addicting, as those who come to depend upon it know. In the Bohemian circles of Munch's day, substance abuse, including alcohol and morphine, were fixtures among the libertines who embraced this lifestyle of creative sadness. Perhaps narcoticizing oneself in the name of inspiration is placating initially. In time, however, it loses its charms. For the most desperate sadness is the one whose desperation is no longer edgy. When all distance has been eliminated between the sadness and the one who continues to bear it, and so they coincide entirely, there is no space for stylization, no room to adopt a pose, no way to inspect it or to mold it, then it is just sadness full stop. Reminiscent of the brooding thinker of Rodin's gates of hell, Munch himself admitted to the existence of those quiet moments when our thought turns inevitably to what may lie beyond this life, to whether there are consequences in the hereafter for how we are living now: "God—and everything was overthrown—everyone raging in a wild, deranged dance of life [....] But I could not set myself free from my fear of life and thoughts of eternal life." Somehow, no matter how hard we may try to avoid it, events thwart our attempt to forget eternity, and call us back to ourselves.

For the artist himself, one such event was the death of his religiously devout father in 1889. In *Night in Saint-Cloud* (1890), the figure of a young man, Munch's roommate, but with whom anybody having undergone his own night watch can immediately empathize, sits in solitude on a couch, staring out the window to the Seine from his shadowy, dark blue room. It will be recalled that, like Munch, the Russian expressive painter Wassily Kandinsky held art should show what we feel when seeing, not merely the objects that one sees. Kandinsky observed how blue of all the colors has the strongest associations with eternity. In Munch's room, the shining turquoise night sky casts a substantial cross-shaped shadow on the floor through the window pane, a symbol of the painter's late father's faith. Having died, where is he now? To where has he crossed over? The room, empty and still, is anything but joyous, yet neither is it despondent, for there is a sweetness to the stillness, an enveloping atmosphere pregnant with a slight, tender hope. Our thinker has reached the "midnight hour," the moment of decision concerning how to respond to God, not just in the face of present bereavement or even a full accounting of the past, but with an eye to the future, given this intense reminder of his own mortality. When we listen to these silences, God speaks to us, gently coaxing us back from the sea of confusion to the shores of clarity through the event that has encountered us. This is a nocturnal moment of reflection, yes, but a vigil too.

It is not a strain to imagine our thinker of Saint-Cloud wondering how those he knows might take his own death. Would all the fellow artists, his audience, his friends and family, feel the absence? Would it even be a loss to them? And if it is conceivable that our own slipping out of the world and joining the dead would hardly cause a stir, is it because those we know are too callous and self-absorbed, or is it rather because, truth be told, we have failed to live a good life that would deservingly lead us to be missed? In the young man's situation, we see how thinking on somebody else's death can turn us to thoughts of our own, and, before we know it, we are making an exacting inventory of our interpersonal affairs in the here and the now. As Rodin's *The Three Shades* shows, often relationships in life, apparent friendships included, are really little more than death pacts. Rodin's figures clasp hands, unified in their shared decision to live the self-interested existence, the life of desire, of lust, one inevitably deteriorating into a dance of envy, jealousy, hatred, and all the anguish, sorrow, and anxiety coming with it. Originally, perhaps there seemed to be strength in the numbers. The shades, though, come to find actually that in the coliseum of lusts, there is just isolation and opposition, a war of all against all in the trivial battle to affirm themselves in the eyes of others. An insecure, pleading desire desiring the validation of others who for their own part only hate themselves, nothing more!

Completed as part of his project *The Frieze of Life*, Munch's *The Dance of Life* (1899–1900) expresses the logic of this desire's progression so well. In it, we see how time takes its toll on those who live lustfully. Judged strictly by the lights of romantic desire, Munch suggests, the stages on life's way lead to nowhere ultimately, and with considerable disaffection along the way! A woman is shown, first as a young virgin in white standing on the foreground's left, then as a wife in red dancing with a male suitor to be her husband, and finally again alone on the foreground's right as a widow in black. She is hollowed out from within by desire's harrowing, a progressive series of painful, confusing experiences propelled by lust, and all of the tumultuous romances to which it gives rise. The passions, so we see, are a dance, effervescent vapors appearing for a brief moment, eventually to be dissipated into thin air by time which blows them all away. Munch's message, perhaps, is that life inevitably leads to cynicism.

A response to the dance of desire and the bitter isolation to which Munch suggests it leads, is to digest experience, turning it into substance for artistic expression. Nothing is particularly harmless about this experiment, since, very often, as Munch's own young torrid romantic life attested, the artistic attitude that seeks creative inspiration in its surroundings always with an eye to tragedy leads to treating others as props, as figures forced unwittingly to participate in some dramatic staging the painter hopes later to distil onto canvass. The consequence is not so much "life as art," for indulging the artistic impulse too zealously truncates life itself into a series of manipulated events, to be curated in a narrative configuration that only bears the all too heavy hand of the artist. People, places, and things end up being put to serve whatever synthetic role the painter has assigned them within his economy of desire and creative vision, the former with an eye to what he knows will later satisfy the latter's autobiographical need for subjects in his painterly confessions and self-explorations. When somebody encounters the artist in the flesh, should she already be a potential future study, a useful metaphor or captivating character in his struggle to come to terms with the torments of his past, and his inner life? The keen powers of intuition and feeling, in Munch's early period, never rose above the aimless desire bereft of any target, and all the emotional turmoil that ensues. Rather than his work expressing a desire that has transcended the attempt to find contentment in itself, an accomplishment that would have required a tranquility of mind and spirit leaving behind the miseries born of lust, he instead elevated the art he created on the wings of anguish to an absolute. As mysterious and beautiful as it is, Munch's is a space that, for all its limitlessness, has something ultimately claustrophobic about it.

If it can be said of Munch's Saint-Cloud thinker that he is lost in thought, it is so because thought itself has the capacity to lure us into a labyrinth from which it becomes progressively difficult to extricate ourselves. Thinking about others will sometimes do this. In *Kiss by the Window* (1892), Munch shows a man and woman kissing at a window overlooking the street. Pressed up against the wall, a curtain to their right, the lovers have entered a private entanglement, invisible to the peering eyes of everybody else. The same enchanting teals and turquoises having charged the room in *Night in Saint-Cloud* are present here again too. In fact, it is not difficult to imagine the solitary man who had been engaged in thinking being the same man who now has joined the dance of life, looking for wholeness, not in the peace of God that had fleetingly touched him in the still room, but now instead in romantic desire. The lovers' unison is transient, a flittering experience the feeling of which the two will seek in vain to find again. Voluptuousness is a desire seeking to repeat itself, and so the original experience to which it gave rise; henceforth, the romance becomes a matter of chasing ephemera. Five years later, 1897's *The Kiss* shows lovers locking lips, but rather than a bright moonlight shining into a room of serene and dreamy blues pregnant with potential, reality has intruded starkly, dashing the lovers' fantasy that their romantic union could be their salvation. Clasping onto one another, straining as if to sustain the dream of fulfillment their lust had appeared to once promise, our two lovers are now in the middle of the foreground, no longer melting into their surroundings, but beginning slowly to contort, congealing into a tangled mass harried by a red and gray and brown wall. Nor does ideality promise anything more abiding or stable. Thoughts of love, whether the memory of old romances or else daydreams concerning the current one, do not satisfy the desire that initiated them.

These lovers occupy a middle point along the arch of desire, noticeably closer than before to the damnation depicted in one of Rodin's own works from 1892, the bronze statue *The*

Kiss. Romantic love founded on nothing but lust begins in an intoxicating fusion, to be sure, but it proves to be a union of self-love, a match whereby each seeks a salvation in the other that the lover is of course unable to provide, something bound to lead to their mutual demise. Such is the lesson that Rodin's Paolo and Francesca da Rimini of the *Fugitive Love* (1887) placed on *The Gates of Hell's* right gate learn. The critic Gustave Geffroy said of Rodin's statue the year it debuted: "the group presents the impatient and fierce race of a woman who carries at her back, as if chained, her victim, an inanimate and rigid man. The woman's back sinks, the man's torso flattens, his legs dangle and an arabesque of limbs is drawn." Geffroy's observation is only partially accurate, however. It is not so much that the man is the victim of the woman's seduction, but that both have been seduced by desire, duped by the fantasy of seeking serenity in a life of lust.

In the crisis of conviction, the midnight hour, as it were, God reaches out to us, exposing us to him by rendering it impossible for us to continue hiding from the thought of him. We hear a voice calling us to leave behind what has been troubling us, to relieve ourselves of the anxieties and efforts that are dominating us, to finally break free of the desires that have driven us to emptiness. It is, in short, Christ who speaks: "Come to Me, all you who labor and are heavy laden, and I will give you rest. Take My yoke upon you and learn from Me, for I am gentle and lowly in heart, and you will find rest for your souls. For My yoke is easy and My burden is light" (Matt. 11:28–31). Unlike our lustful desires, here is a kind Master! In order to forget the opportunity God has extended us to start over, it will be necessary to silence all memory of the encounter, including all conscious trace of this very decision itself to have rebuffed it. The dance of life, the game of desire, God had temporarily interrupted in turn recommences, this time with more vigor than before, so that we might let it deafen us to what we have heard in the stillness of the midnight hour. It will be necessary to throw ourselves into a condition as close to oblivion as possible. Deciding not to "Cast all your cares on Him, for He cares for you" (1 Pet. 5:7), that is to say, not turning to Christ, henceforth means plunging ever deeper into the passions, finally, if necessary, to the point of frenzied rebellion, a frantic desire to silence the call that had momentarily neutralized the desires along with all of their vain fantasies, by allowing us to see lucidly how they have disfigured us. Eventually, this conscious pursuit of unconsciousness must become masochistic, for in trying to forget what has encountered us, the one who rejects God's offer of help only wills the deliberate ruination of himself.

Upon looking again, we see the Saint-Cloud thinker blends almost seamlessly into the surroundings, his hat and coat camouflaged by the wall and couch, as if, in this moment of self-emptying, he is nothing at all, just another item of furniture whose human pride has been nullified by the infinite gaze of God staring down from high above him. Rodin's shades, of course, are not so self-effacing at all. Instead, these are figures consciously adopting a posture of defiance in the attempt of asserting their identity through independence, to install themselves as bulwarks opposing the divine will, fixtures of rebellion resisting the God who has offended their pride. Creatures who resent their being creatures, and who consequently resent their Creator!

Necessarily, doing what they desire to do will require banishing the memory of God as thoroughly as they can, since God's presence would spoil their illusion, ruining the notion that they are more than just men. As Paul says, "And even as they did not like to retain God in their knowledge, God gave them over to a reprobate mind, to do those things which are not convenient" (Rom. 1:28). What had begun as the attempt to satisfy desires aiming at finite ends, in short, a life that transforms as it progresses into one of competition with others, hereby crosses into territory that is knowingly demonic. Now, the previously masochistic life of frustrated desire that had tried to resign itself to disappointment but had always been tinged with an undercurrent of malice for others because of that frustration, blossoms into unbridled hate of God and so others, the black flower of pure sadism.

Fueled by a rejection of God so complete that it prefers damnation to abandoning the lusts it knows is leading it there, this economy of desire finally relinquishes itself to the kingdom of spite. For evil, the last vestige of justice ends in a perfect inversion of what justice truly is: from the deranged perspective of the condemned shade, it is unfair for God to punish him for the desire that has led him to be unable to live without it. For the shade, good is simply getting what he wants, and bad is being denied it. Consequently, for God to hold him accountable for doing what he desires is to wrong him, the shade! This, then, is the darkened mind of the one alienated from God, the one lost in a fog, in a raging storm of seething desires.

If the life of the passions, the life of untamed desire, leads to self-willed destruction, it is for this reason that God, in love, commands us to be set free from it. As John's Gospel says, "So if the Son sets you free, you will be free indeed" (John 8:32). The passage to freedom, to the joyful peace otherwise eluding desire, lies in self-abnegation. Paul perhaps says it best, when, in the midst of a discussion explaining the difference between the flesh and the Spirit, he says to those in Galatia: "And they that are Christ's have crucified the flesh with the affections and lusts" (Gal. 5:24). For the second half of his life, Munch lived alone in isolation, dedicating himself to his work, his eye frequently turning to the landscape. In earlier works like *Starry Night* (1893), *Winter* (1899), or *New Snow* (1900), we see a tranquility absent in the psychological works from the same period exploring the human dance of life in all its torrid anguishes and lusts. To be sure, it is possible to quell desire, so that it no longer strives in vain to devour itself in the excesses of alcohol, or drugs, or lust—as Munch himself learned, artistic creation can serve as an outlet, in part, for the ravages of desire. As these landscapes of his remind us, nature's beauty provides key assistance in this, since its serenity offers us a model to imitate. And yet, in this transition from wild excess to constrained stability, the relative satisfaction that results still remains more of a deflation than a fulfillment. Munch's paintings seem to point powerfully to a desire whose last gesture is resignation, a great sigh. Youth's wish is to satisfy itself with what to it at the time seemed possible. God feels unnecessary. In time, by the end, with nothing left to look forward to, this wish has become exhausted desire's deepest need—to die alone, without God.

Chapter 4

The Golden Calf

What usually do we treasure besides what we think is, or should be, ours? And what, moreover, could be dearer to us in this respect than our very own identity, what others see when they encounter us, and so presumably come accordingly to know us? To be sure, we can spend a significant portion of each day engaged in some way dealing with the challenge of shaping ourselves, there being a thousand different little ways by which we try to sculpt ourselves, to form self-knowledge through a detour, through what the perception or opinion of others provides. However, in the pursuit of what Martin Heidegger and others term authenticity, so frequently we only fail, succumbing instead to a conformist existence, a mere shadow of our true or best selves, a failure whose form takes shape from the inundation of second-hand knowledge we receive about ourselves from others, from the reactions we get to the self-image that we have projected, the face we have shown to the world, the response to which will determine that self-conception's success or failure. Today, this exteriorization of self is for us conventional. Without the slightest hesitation, we entrust ourselves to the crowd, placing our identity in the hands of others, letting their attitudes and beliefs about us shape us so fundamentally. Whatever else may be said of the self-image that doing so forges, there is hardly anything, if anything at all, of God in it. It is thus with an eye to this stubborn slippage of substituting finite things for God that Christ in his Sermon on the Mount instructs those listening (and us as well) to seek one's identity, and thus treasure, in heavenly things: "Lay up for yourselves treasures in heaven, where neither moth nor rust doth corrupt, and where thieves do not break through nor steal:

For where your treasure is, there shall be your heart also" (Matt. 6:20–21).

What happens when the heart strays, wandering after what it happens to treasure more than God? This is the question a venerable tradition of classicist paintings puts to us. Painted sometime between 1633 and 1634, and taking the biblical account of Moses and the Israelites' Exodus from Egypt as its subject, Nicolas Poussin's *The Adoration of the Golden Calf* is one such example, an iconic Baroque study in idolatry. However, it would be premature to dismiss its narrative as little more than mythological storytelling, as if it were a work whose moralizing theme can perhaps serve as a quaint reminder not to place undue importance on life's small things, to keep things in perspective, to prioritize our interests proportionately, but nothing more. To the contemporary eye, Poussin's work is not seen to be offering us anything like a fundamental transcendental insight into the human condition, and so for us today. We exempt ourselves from the drama, skimming along the surface, content to take in the scene before us as though it were something we can keep at arm's distance, something consigned to an ancient, or better, simply mythical past. With a condescending sense of assured knowing, we might mistake ourselves to be above anything it has to teach us. But if the frolicking Israelites surrounding the calf look so foolish to us, is not their own bizarre behavior the inevitable outcome of the adoration that adores something absolutely other than God? Do we today not do the same? Why, then, are we so quick to assume we are immune in principle from such folly? Is not there something just as buffoonish about those today hypnotically dancing for a TikTok video, or pursing their lips and flexing their muscles for an Instagram image? No matter how great and commonplace such behavior becomes in the technological era of social media, there is no denying we are in bizarre times, indeed, when publicly sharing a photograph of one's lunch or dinner is considered to be interesting. As it happens, this is a perennial bizarreness. As we shall see, idolatry did not used to exist only later to disappear with us, nor has it come onto the scene just recently. It has subsisted without respite, and so it persists today.

Overcoming the false prejudice that we have advanced beyond our forebears to the point of now being immune from the risk of repeating their errors again ourselves, and so now turning to the Poussin with a humble look willing to see, what then do we see? The Book of Exodus characterizes the scene as being an obnoxious one to Moses. Having ascended Mount Sinai, he at "the finger of God" (Ex. 31:18) has just received the Ten Commandments on two stone tablets. Making his way off the mountain for what he expects will be a crowd anticipating his return, he hears a great commotion coming from the Israelite camp he's left in Aaron's charge. As he approaches, he finds to his horror everyone dancing around a golden calf, the false god whom they have installed to replace the God who had delivered them from Pharaoh's Egypt by having parted the Red Sea. The Septuagint relates the history:

> Wisdom entered into the soul of the servant of the Lord, and withstood dreadful kings in wonders and signs; rendered to the righteous a reward of their labours, guided them in a marvellous way, and was unto them for a cover by day, and a light of stars in the night season; brought them through the Red sea, and led them through much water: but she drowned their enemies, and cast them up out of the bottom of the deep. Therefore the righteous spoiled the ungodly, and praised thy holy name, O Lord, and magnified with one accord thine land, that fought for them. For wisdom opened the mouth of the dumb, and made the tongues of them that cannot speak eloquent. She prospered their works in the hand of the holy prophet. They went through the wilderness that was not inhabited, and pitched tents in places where

there lay no way. They stood against their enemies, and were avenged of their adversaries. When they were thirsty, they called upon thee, and water was given them out of the flinty rock, and their thirst was quenched out of the hard stone. (Wisdom X.16–XI.8)

Such ungratefulness, in turn, from Israel! Poussin shows Moses, a puny figure in the background, in ambiguous motion, God's law lifted in his two hands across his chest and above his right shoulder. Is this still for him a moment of triumph raising the tablets so as to draw attention to them, or is he already enraged by what he has discovered, and so readying to smash the tablets to pieces on the ground in a fury? At any rate, Moses is ignored by nearly everyone, with nobody except one woman standing on the edge of the crowd turning her head around to look at him, and perhaps another woman, who, closer to the calf, shoots a stunned look of consternation towards him. Moses looks rather like the parent who has come home from a trip early, to have caught the children doing something they should not be doing. What should be a moment of collective celebration for Moses and the people over everything the God of Israel has done for them, including now the bestowal of the Ten Commandments, is instead disrupted, drowned out in the cacophony of revelry. Everything appears against an unsettling sundown light the faint orange and red hue of which, in keeping with the voluptuous exuberance rippling through the wild crowd (many of whom are wearing red and orange garments matching the sky), forebodingly portends the coming wrath of God.

Of course, this is not the first time God will have come to punish mankind in his holy disappointment. God's giving of the Ten Commandments to Moses follows on a series of events in the story of his covenant with the Israelites. And when the tribes of Israel break that covenant, God judges them for it, albeit ultimately with an eye to their correction. But even well before this relationship is established, God takes an active role in human affairs, beginning with the very first days of creation. In *Spring* or *The Earthly Paradise* (1660–64), Poussin turns back to Eden, revealing Adam and Eve at the moment of their decision to transgress the commandment not to eat of the tree of the knowledge of good and evil. Nestled snugly within an orchard surrounded by lush foliage, a pond, and pristine hills, Eve is seen pointing to the tree of forbidden fruit, her arm grabbing Adam to draw his attention to what has caught her eye. The husband, sitting on his backside, elbow resting on his knee, stares into his wife's face with a look of dumb eagerness. As for God, whom Poussin depicts as a figure on a cloud, he can be seen already in full flight, abandoning Adam and Eve to face the consequences of their imminent disobedience. This is now a paradise lost.

Wholly in contrast to this scene of human disobedience and divine judgment stands a long classicist tradition, of which Poussin's own work played a considerable part, works recounting an alternative image of human history, one offering a mythical account of our origins making no reference to the judgment of God. It is an idyllic, enchanted history erasing the least trace of any primordial fall. As a look at the indicative Claude Lorrain's *Seaport with the Embarkation of the Queen of Sheba* (1648) reveals unabashedly, such a perspective conceives human life to be an odyssey of desire. For although the scene before us concerns the Old Testament story of Queen of Sheba's journey to visit King Solomon in Jerusalem for his legendary reputation for wisdom, everything about it is poetic, above all the prominent sea horizon accentuating the painting's suggestion of a distant imaginary land laying beyond what meets the eye. The bustling port is blanketed by a bright sunlight, the gentle dark blue waves reflecting the light's majestic rays, the surrounding buildings with their imposing steps and ornate columns all befitting a regal kingdom. There is not the faintest intimation of suffering or strife. The magisterial kingdom evidently subsists as if unseen by the gaze of God, somehow exempted from the world's evils and the shadow of sin and death. A friend of Lorrain's, the Italian painter Salvator Rosa depicts a similarly cheerful scene in his *Port Marina* (1640), a lighthouse standing on the distant edge of a serene harbor illuminated under the light of a white sun, cumulous clouds dawdling over the sea, providing an amusing distraction for the happy people bustling about their work in port. The impressive castle on the foreground's left, rising above the docked ships, basks in the glow of the expansive sunset, a fortress whose stature provides the city's inhabitants a vantage point from which to stare off to sea, content to know that a rosy future awaits them here in something approximating paradise. It is this same Edenic atmosphere figuring in Lorrain's and Rosa's works that appears once again in 1874's *The Port of Bordeaux* by Eugène Bordin. Here, however, everything is far less grandiose, more directly relatable. A simple seascape blurring the boundaries between sea and sky, it presents a handful of modest sailboats propelled gently by the breeze. There are no visible human figures at work, just a welcoming tranquility. Whereas Lorrain and Rosa represent their sea harbors as loci of monumental labor and epic voyages, places of adventure open to alluringly mysterious destinations, Bordin instead makes the port itself the destination. Would anybody on one of these boats or walking the dock want to leave the bay's serene confines? Rather than inciting our penchant for exploration, Bordin captures the experience of being content with where we are, as if our present surroundings could suffice forever.

At the beginning of an incredibly perceptive analysis of one of Poussin's bacchanals, the American art historian Richard T. Neer quotes the following description of *The Birth of Bacchus* (1657) from a biography of Poussin written by the artist's own friend, the seventeenth-century theorist Giovanni Pietro Bellori, who writes,

> The baby whom Mercury presents to that Nymph is the newly-born Bacchus. The nymph is Dirce, daughter of the river who receives him joyfully and admires the divinely born child. She is embraced about the shoulder by another Nymph, who points out the infant to the accompanying Naiads, who, seated in the water, turn in curiosity and gaze admiringly at him. Behold Jupiter in the clouds above, reclining in bed where he gave birth to the child, and with him Hebe ministering ambrosia to him as a restorative. But it is the cave by the river that is wholly prodigious, for it is clothed in new vine leaves and new grapes interlaced with ivy, born at the birth of Bacchus. The god Pan sits on the hills above, joyfully on the sonorous reeds of his pipes, and the same image was also painted by Philostratus. The other figures in the corner of the painting are no part of this fable, because the painter, following the description and sequence of Ovid's *Metamorphoses*, continued with another fable, that of Narcissus, who through love of himself ended in death, and the painting shows him dead next to the water in which he used to mirror himself. He lies crowned with the flowers into which he was changed, and Echo sits nearby him, miserably enamored, who, leaning on her upper arm, by her harsh pallor perfectly appears transformed into stone.[7]

As Neer further observes, "Poussin's narrative derives its authority, and to some extent its intelligibility, from Ovid: but it is not Ovid's narrative,"[8] for its intelligibility stems from the work's visibility as such, and not the philosophical or textual sources upon which it is associated or upon which it has drawn. Paintings exhibit their own form of integrity, and hence are irreducible to the rhetorical narratives that may happen to have inspired them. Nor is a painting's treatment of a particular subject reducible to other paintings having come before it. Later in the analysis, for instance, Neer notes the various ways by which Poussin's scene creatively appropriates Titian's own work on the same subject, *The Bacchanal of the Andrians* (1518– 19). Underlying Poussin's vision is an overarching commitment to the idea that artistic creation, which he believed to consist in *mimesis,* must nevertheless resist lapsing into a copying realism. Reworking a well-worn theme addressed by Titian and many others, he successfully demonstrates the classicist thesis of a past that is never exhausted, by showing how something new and singular—his reimagined depictions of the familiar stories of Bacchus and Narcissus, in this case—can emerge through creative *mimesis.*

Poussin, as it happens, detested the work of his near contemporary Caravaggio for representing everything he took to be wrong with pure realism. Poussin's personal dislike notwithstanding, Caravaggio's own encounter with Ovid in the form of his rendition of *Narcissus* (1597–99) is certainly worthy of remark. As the *Metamorphoses* itself recounts, Narcissus is the handsome youth who Ovid tells us falls in love with himself. Staring dreamily into the reflection of his image, he eventually dies and departs to Styx. In Caravaggio, Narcissus kneels at the edges of a dark pool, his arms bracing himself as he leans down for a closer look, lips parted, poised for a kiss. Here is a ghastly sacrifice, to offer oneself on the altar of self-glorification—an insular act that ends, predictably, in the self-inflicted mutilation of one's own being. This is more than mythology. Narcissus, in fact, is the ancient predecessor of what for us has become rampant, a transcendental egoism consisting in the illusion of independence and self-sufficiency from God, a shallow pride leading to the pursuit of glamor and prestige and ultimately the cult of self-adoration, thereby culminating in an existence whereby one becomes one's own idol, one's own golden calf. Paul has in mind something along these lines, a self-exaltation leaving no room for God owing to its having installed oneself as a god, when he denounces the self-idolatry of the antichrist. The description he offers of such a figure fits anybody who, as Narcissus, worships himself: "Who opposeth, and exalteth himself above all that is called God: so that he as God sitteth in the temple of God, shewing himself as though he were God" (2 Thess. 2:4). For Paul, the most pernicious of all graven images is the self-image that has taken itself as its own object of gaze, the image resulting when one idolatrously worships a glorified reflection of oneself.

Underlying the hedonistic frenzy shown by Poussin is the decision to have thrown oneself headlong into whatever path desire opens. As the Book of Wisdom explains it, the Dionysian life plunges itself into excess as a response to the death it knows always already renders everything it desires so fleeting. Contrary to widespread portrayal, paganism is not a form of existence affirming life on earth naïvely and fully. Its surface exuberance only veils a profound inner movement of resignation with which it began, the relinquishment of all hope:

For the ungodly said, reasoning with themselves, but not aright, Our life is short and tedious, and in the death of a man there is no remedy: neither was there any man known to have returned from the grave. For we are born at all adventure: and we shall be hereafter as though we had never been: for the breath in our nostrils is as smoke, and a little spark in the moving of our heart: which being extinguished, our body shall be turned to ashes, and our spirit shall vanish as the soft air, and our name shall be forgotten in time, and no man shall have our works in remembrance, and our life shall pass away as the trace of a cloud, and shall be dispersed as a mist, that is driven away with the beams of the sun, and overcome with the heat thereof. For our time is a very shadow that passeth away: and after our end there is no returning: for it is fast sealed, so that no man cometh again. Come on therefore, let us enjoy the good things that are present: and let us speedily use the creatures with costly wine and ointments: and let no flower of the spring pass by us. Let us crown ourselves with rosebuds, before they be withered: let none of us go without his part of our voluptuousness: let us leave tokens of our joyfulness in every place: for this is our portion, and our lot is this. (Wisdom II.1–9)

From the perspective of the Dionysian reveler living for the moment, and so enjoyment, this is the hope of hopelessness: may there be only this mortal life with its enjoyments, and then irrevocable death! Thus, for those living at the time of the Book of Wisdom's writing, it was feasible perhaps to try to console themselves with the thought that there will not be anything beyond the grave, for, just as was observed above, nobody theretofore had ever returned from the grave. The heart of the matter emerges. It is evil's twisted desire to remain unaccountable for its deeds in life that God eliminates, so decisively once and for all, with the raising of Jesus from the dead. Paul will later convey the message to the Greeks: "And the times of this ignorance God winked at: but now commandeth all men everywhere to repent. Because he will judge the world in righteousness by that man whom he hath ordained: whereof he that has given assurance unto all men, in that he hath raised him from the dead" (Acts 17:30–31). Without having to invoke the event of the resurrection, it is still possible to note that as weightless as such whimsicality may feel for a time, eventually it returns down to earth, and not without consequences.

In 1767's *The Swing*, the French Rococo painter and printmaker Jean-Honoré Fragonard depicts the intrigues characterizing the kind of embarrassing situations to which unbridled hedonism gives rise. Bursting with rhapsody, everything seems to be swelling from within itself, expanding from an undercurrent of erotic desire. In the midst of an enchanted garden, a young woman in pink and white rides a swing hanging from a tree, her dress billowing as she careens through the air. To the left lies a man concealed on his back in the bushes, his left arm outstretched to pave a view so that he is able to see up the woman's dress. His is not the gaze of some unwanted peeper, but rather one who has taken her as his mistress. Clearly, the two are well-acquainted. Meanwhile, the woman's elderly and unsuspecting husband stands off in the background pushing the swing, totally oblivious to the other man's presence and his wife's infidelity. This is a secret garden of sorts, for it is a secret space between lovers, a hidden desire by which they devour one another unbeknown to others. A statue is above the adulterer lying in the bush, a small angelic stone figure holding its finger to its lips in the sign of silence. Fragonard captures the distinctive mood of pagan elation, the intoxicating sense of relief those who take themselves to be liberated from God feel. If their affair is a secret garden for these two lovers, it is because it is experienced as a purely human situation, one without any God to intrude and to hold them to account.

While Lorrain's and Rosa's seascapes occasioned thoughts of a desire setting out on a journey to some great distant land, Gustave Guillaumet represents that journey's end as one of doom, as symbolized by the husk of a once formidable desire that has died of thirst in the desert. His 1867's *The Sarhara, or the Desert* in the Musée d'Orsay shows a solitary dead animal decomposing in the desolation of a desert heat. Guillaumet's painting is a cautionary reminder of how desire is not so harmless. The direction in which it points us, if taken, can lead to a journey ending badly. Paul, for one, makes just this point in a letter to his protégé Timothy, when he comments on the fact of how our desires can ensnare us, especially greed: "But they that will be rich fall into temptation and a snare, and into many foolish and hurtful lusts, which drown men in destruction and perdition. For the love of money is the root of all evil: which while some coveted after they have erred from the faith and pierced themselves through with many sorrow" (1 Tim. 6:9–10). Here Peter Paul Rubens' *The Tribute Money* (1612–1614) in San Francisco's Legion of Honor is worth considering. Rubens shows the famous confrontation between Christ and the minions (Luke's term is "spies") sent by the Pharisees. The scheme, we read in Matthew, is to entrap Christ by catching him encouraging the Jews not to pay taxes owed to the Romans, an offense of sedition against the civil authorities that the Pharisees hope will in turn have Christ arrested and delivered to Pilate. Standing in the composition's right, Christ points skyward with his left arm, his other hand extending coins to one of the perplexed men before him. In response to their question regarding whether it is right for the people of Israel to pay such taxes, Christ says, "Render unto Caesar the things that are Caesar's, and unto God the things that are God's" (Matt. 22:21). The coin's specific identity remains a matter of dispute. Perhaps it was a denarius featuring the image of Tiberius. In any case, the lesson is clear. Christ in no way disputes any worldly authority's proper claim over taxes and its kingdom of mammon. He concedes all that precisely in order to point out its paltriness in comparison to God's kingdom. Paying the tax as a complete afterthought, Christ treats it as a triviality. Money, he suggests, is worthless! In an earlier encounter with the Pharisees also manifesting this same eternal sense of proportion, Christ had said God is interested in obtaining our heart, not any other outward sacrifice, and certainly not money: "Well hath Esaias prophesied of you hypocrites, as it is written, This people honoureth me with their lips, but their heart is far from me" (Mark 7:6). If our true treasure should be in heaven, then it is nothing to give away what is lesser, the money carnal men consumed by their earthly affairs mistake for treasure. Let them have their money! God wants us to render our very selves to him, a tribute far weightier and more precious than any trifling affair to do with money.

What has contaminated the Temple in Jerusalem is not merely greed, however, or even hypocrisy. At work is something the perniciousness of which is far more sinister: a demonic cabal of those who have not only departed from God, but has sworn its allegiance to oppose God by serving Satan instead. This is what Christ will elsewhere call the "synagogue of Satan" (Rev 2:9 and Rev 3:9). As Alexander Hislop's underappreciated nineteenth-century tome *The Two Babylons* recounts in painstaking detail, rather than monotheism having arisen from earlier polytheistic traditions, the pagan Babylonian, Greek, Roman, and other gods enact the one and same mystery religion, one commemorating the Tower of Babel's Nimrod. What the Greeks know as Hermes or the Romans know as Mercury, for instance, is in fact Cush, the father of the Nimrod who hated the God of Israel, the rebellious grandson of Ham and great-grandson of Noah.

Hence, truth be told, both the idyllic view of human history and the romantic image of ancient paganism accompanying it are fable. Ancient festivals and their rites were not always so kind to everyone involved. Often, they involved horrendous violence, including human sacrifice. In his *On the Genealogy of Morals*, Friedrich Nietzsche in the work's First Essay claims to trace our common, everyday morality's conception of good and evil—what he calls "herd" or "slave" morality—back to an impotent thirst for the revenge of the weak (the slaves or the "lambs") against the stronger (the masters or the "eagles"). In turn, there follows a negation and inversion of what had been the more primitive values among the strong and noble, and the so-called "master morality" is overthrown. At the heart of the master values, says Nietzsche, was a desire to inflict cruelty. As he states, "*Cruelty* constituted the great festival pleasure of more primitive men and was indeed an ingredient of almost every one of their pleasures."[9] Entirely psychologizing

Nietzsche's ambiguous genealogical thesis, Freud for his own part in *Civilization and its Discontents* claimed to discover a fundamental psychic drive within us, a "death drive" compelling us to dominate and to destroy. Without meaning in the least to downplay the reality of these dark tendencies in human life, it must be emphasized that, no matter what Nietzsche or Freud may say, the lusts to cruelty and domination are disturbances of proper psychic human functioning, instances of a disordered mind, a mind that has lost touch with God, and so the light.

Rosa's own 1646 painting *Witches at their Incantations* illuminates this shadow world of darkness. In the early morning hours, a witch coven goes about its wicked business, while tucked away in some secluded black hills far away from any prying eyes. A trio sits on the ground, grinding away at human bones they're preparing for a cannibalistic stew. To the left, two men sit next to a skeleton drafting up some script of incantations. A man standing behind the seated trio brandishes a bloody sword, as a woman nearby carries a swaddled baby who appears to be the rite's next sacrifice.

Only a profound ignorance (if it is sincere) could dismiss this existence of such wickedness as simply the stuff of Rosa's Gothic imagination. In reality, what those in the throes of the heart of darkness are capable of doing goes well beyond the scopes of mere cruelty, and becomes truly diabolic. There is the criminal mind that leads to offenses violating the laws and customs of its civil society. And then there is the demonic mind that leads to felonies against creation itself, acts that make us shudder, acts that can only be explained as intended to deface reality, to violate human dignity, and to spite God himself by trying to give him a bad name. These are the things which, when revealed, lead some to wonder whether there is a God. In *The Brothers Karamazov*, the middle brother Ivan, an anguished doubter, recounts his morbid practice of reading through the newspapers to ruminate over all of the repugnant things that have been done, things so terrible that Ivan says thinking on them is what has led him to "give back his ticket," to disown this world because of its evil, even if there is a God who has created it. Later on, Ivan has what literary interpreters deem a hallucinatory encounter with the devil. However, such a reading probably is too quick to dismiss the possibility that Dostoevsky intends for the encounter to be understood as being veridical. As it happens, Dostoevsky himself took the demonic to be very real, and he thought it had a hand in everyday human events. Scoff initially as we might at the suggestion, these are the evils that defy any hypothesis other than that they have originated in a pact with the devil. As the police, prosecutors, psychologists, and other court officials concede, far from these being the actions of someone insane, these are calculated and exacting actions, crimes carried out according to their own perverse logic of control, domination, and cruelty. They are crimes meant to break the soul of the victim, and disturb anyone who comes to learn of them, monuments erected to exalt the power of darkness responsible for having given rise to them, a power detesting everything except for the glee it derives in satisfying its diabolic lust to humiliate, violate, and crush others. In short, these are events bearing witness to an enemy of humanity come "to steal, and to kill, and to destroy" (John 10:10).

In *Crime and Punishment*, Dostoevsky tells the story of Raskolnikov, a troubled young student who, taken in and overcome by his dark fantasies of murder, kills two women with a hammer. The account of Raskolnikov is inspired by the sort of events that haunt Ivan Karamazov, events that happen today. The two Ukrainian teenagers Igor Suprunyuck and Viktor Sayenko, known as the "Dnipropetrovsk Maniacs," serve as a case in point. For them, the sadistic pleasure delighting itself in destroying purity and innocence began with abusing animals. They kill and mutilate a dog, hanging its corpse from a tree limb. They pose for photographs, smiling about and laughing at what they have done. From there, it will be necessary to try torture. A kitten is selected, nailed to a cross, and made to whimper as it struggles for its life pitifully. When the boys are bored and have seen enough, finally they shoot it with pistols. Other animals meet similar fates, while the boys develop the habit of drawing swastikas on the walls in blood as they pose with the carcasses. The twisted compulsion to satisfy their sadistic rush only deepens, and so the craving to torment others expands its horizons. It does not take long before the victims are human beings. Over the span of four weeks in summer, the boys go on a killing spree, bludgeoning innocent bystanders to death with a hammer they rap in a yellow bag. Everything is recorded on camera and photographed. A murdered pregnant woman has her baby cut out of the womb. A man is knocked from his bike, his face smashed in with the hammer, a screwdriver driven through his eyes as he ineffectually fights for life. The boys all the while talk casually to each other during the torture and murder, as if it is nothing. When they are done, they laugh in astonishment at how the man struggled for his life for as long as he did, wipe off the blood, make Nazi salutes over the corpse, and leave the body in the roadside wood. By the time the reign of terror is stopped with their arrest, twenty-one people are dead. At the trial, the court decides they have killed simply for fun, to enjoy the depraved high of terrifying others who were helpless. Be that as it may be, it is not quite right. For it omits something crucial. For why did the boys film everything? The court never develops a plausible explanation. Some with direct knowledge of the case put forward the idea that the boys had been hired to film the murders after having agreed to make what would in turn be distributed as online snuff films. Such an underworld does exist. For example, the serial killer, kidnapper, and rapist Marc Paul Alain Dutroux kept a basement dungeon where he would hold young girls to be tortured, raped, and murdered. It has been alleged others would visit the dungeon, to be able to have their way with the imprisoned victims. At one location, the ring of abusers tie a young girl with rope in such a way that when she struggled to escape, she strangled herself, a contraption which the satanic mind who devised it no doubt found clever and funny. Many powerful people—politicians, businessmen, and so forth—are implicated. In the face of appalling government corruption in the investigation, 300,000 Belgians took to the streets in the White March. As the Dutroux Affair shows, there exists a criminal syndicate profiting from the production and distribution of films showing the rape, torture, and killing of children. The naïve and gullible public who learns of these evils is quick to suppress the memory of what has been revealed to it, discounting the possibility that the devil could really have been at work in such things. But as for those themselves who operate in this satanic underworld, the prince of darkness is real. They know, because they serve him.

Contrary, then, to what a certain line of naïve secularism common today would contend, evil does not call God's existence into question. Rather, it renders that existence more undeniable. Evils so horrendous as those recounted above are only intelligible as the repudiations of God they are, evils committed in opposition to God's goodness, and done in allegiance to the devil. In the face of this demonic wickedness, one can understand God's anger. Commissioned by the Duc de Richelieu to create a panel of the four seasons, Poussin in his last years selected the biblical theme of the flood for the series' winter subject. Whereas the spring piece, the aforementioned study of Adam and Eve in the garden, was ambiguous insofar as it celebrated nature's fertility, here Poussin depicts the consequences for idolatry in uncompromising terms, the price to pay for having indulged the excesses of unfettered desire, a desire that losing sight of God, consequently lost sight of the good. A bolt of lightning tears through the work's black sky, as desperate figures flee for dry ground. One man clasps his hands together above his head, raising them to the heavens, pleading with God for mercy as his boat goes under. A body floats in the rapids nearby. To the right, a woman clinging to driftwood charts a course toward a cliff of rocks, as the man behind her sits atop a donkey whose snout is barely above the rising tide. A number of others fight to pull others from the waters into a tottering boat, as they make way to the same rock outcropping. All the while, slithering across the land at the left foreground is a snake, a physical manifestation of the power of darkness that had enticed the people of Israel into forsaking God. Poussin shows that Satan's bid to be equal to the Most High has failed. Judgment has come from the Creator who is fed up with evil. If previously people had been able to convince themselves that life was intended to be a garden of delights, one big reckless odyssey of desire, a marketplace of lusts, a place to do however they pleased, now they know how mistaken they were to think so. In their hubris, those who turn from God believe that they are unseen, that there is safety in the numbers of others who are doing the same: "Say not thou, I will hide myself from the Lord: shall any remember me from above? I shall not be remembered among so many people: for what is my soul among such an infinite number of creatures?" (Ecclus. XVI.17). But as the same text continues, this is wishful thinking: "None of their unrighteous deeds are hid from him, but all their deeds are before the Lord" (Ecclus. XVII.20). In a moment, the humanistic mythical image of a world without God is shattered.

What is more profitable, and hence more to be treasured, than being placed beyond the clutches of such evil, shielded in Christ from its powers? Our destiny lies in heaven, our identity in Christ. This is the true gold! As the Septuagint accordingly says when comparing this true gold with mere earthly treasures, "Lay up thy treasure according to the commandments of the most High, and it shall bring the more profit than gold" (Ecclus. XXIX.11). As for the authentic life that struggles unsuccessfully to find its identity in unrestrained desires, inevitably it remains under the sway of darkness.[10] Divorced from the goal of becoming wise, the task of being oneself meets with failure. For, underestimating evil, it fails to take adequate refuge from it. God treasures each of us, and for this reason he has called us to enter into covenant with him. When we do, relinquishing control and handing ourselves over, we find that act of trust rewarded. Following Paul, we can do no better than apply a formula to ourselves expressing the lesson learned from what happened to the Israelites in the wilderness: "We should not lust after evil things, as they also lusted" (1 Cor. 10:6). God's commandments, it turns out, are not meant to spoil our fun or to inhibit our freedom in the name of oppression. They are given for us in love, to protect us from the evil one.

Chapter 5

Through the Veil of the Word Made Flesh

To hand ourselves over completely to the desire for finite things, to entrust our pursuit of fulfillment to the goals and the aspirations for which this desire yearns, only condemns us to inevitable self-frustration. Even our successes are failures. And so, along this way of desire, existence increasingly dissolves into the mists of time. Stretched into exhaustion by worries over the future and by the burdens of the past, the resulting life is scattered, moving perpetually, always embarked on some course to some or other destination, never reaching a stable mooring. For, concerned with how we appear to others, held hostage to the false self we have presented to try to please or appease them, no matter what we accomplish or attain, we consequently find ourselves adrift, launched upon a journey whose cost has been to exact from us the severest of all possible prices, the loss of ourself. If, then, the preceding chapters have aimed to establish one thing, it is to disclose the stupor in which we grope when we are estranged from God, whatever the particular reason is. Having fought for however long it may be to live apart from God, how will coming to know him be achievable after persisting alone? What form can a reconciliation between God and us take?

The incarnation transforms everything, as Caravaggio's *Conversion on the Way to Damascus* (1601) shows. Before the Word took flesh, time possessed no clear meaning, neither for humanity as a whole or each of us individually, but with the incarnation, a new time opens, one not only now measured by eternity, but by a God who himself has entered time, and thereby demonstrated his providence over creation. As for the act of conversion, it is simply then the act of embracing this transformation of the cosmos itself, the acceptance of what has occurred, but was being disregarded by us. For as everyone who is confronted with the event of God having become man in Jesus Christ experiences (and sometimes even the most mundane things of daily life such as dating a check can serve as reminders), time becomes eschatological, human existence is made inherently historical, and with each and every passing year things are referred back incessantly to the event responsible for absolutely rupturing everything that had come before it and has happened afterward. Nothing is still the same in the wake of the incarnation's taking place. Though the change is universal, for it exempts nobody living today, neither is it therefore impersonal. It addresses each of us intimately. And when we encounter it personally as an event interrupting and overturning our sense of what we had till then understood life to be, in a moment, like Paul, we are flattened, jolted awake by the recognition of the immensity of what is now dawning on us, that for all this time we have been sleeping, wandering aimlessly in a dreamworld all the while oblivious to our somnolence, this daily illusion of our own desire's making. In a flash, God reaches us and says, "Let there be light!"

The light illuminates us; it forces us to see ourselves honestly. To be brought to lucidity can be a painful experience, even a trial, as the Book of Acts describes proved to be the case for Paul. Before encountering the risen Christ, Paul was comfortable in his socially acceptable role as Saul of Tarsus. At the time a proud "Pharisee of Pharisees" (Phil. 3:5), his responsibility was to oversee the persecution of Jesus' followers. The author of Hebrews describes how Paul's targets were not at all esteemed like him, but were persecuted, treated as outcasts with disdain. They receive the scorn and attacks they do for belonging to what is called "the way" (Acts 9:2). What way exactly is this? What distinguishes it from alternative ways, this way inciting such passionate opposition from those whom like Paul on his way to Damascus was willing to stop at nothing to stamp it out? The Fourth Gospel notes of it how the way at issue consists in the emulation of a prototype, the one who sets for it the pattern to follow. In this instance, the prototype is none other than the Word, which with the incarnation takes flesh and assumes the human, and thus mortal, condition. Nothing remains the same. The incarnation is essential, for it answers everything regarding what we are to do with our time that leads to death, not least by orienting our understanding of ourselves and our human purpose here on earth in a way that would otherwise have remained obscure. The haze lifts. The riddle dissolves. Life ceases to be a Promethean project of forging an identity by way of the purposes we choose to determine for ourselves. Now, it instead takes on the pure form of a divinely appointed vocation, a task God gives us. Called to enter the kingdom of heaven, an individual's existence finds itself through emulating the way, the way to eternal life in Christ. Henceforth, the incarnation points the way for us, because Christ, while on earth, by dwelling among us, leaves the pattern of life by which reaching eternal life is made possible. In a discussion recounted by the fourteenth chapter of John's Gospel regarding how to obtain such eternal life, Christ in response to a disciple who asks how we are to find it explains that the way to eternal life lies in him, that is to say, through the way of life that finds Life by having recognized the identity of Christ and eternal life. There is nothing abstract involved in making the recognition, for the divinization it in turn calls for in emulating Christ is not a matter of *gnosis*. It rather entails a corresponding transfiguration of desire, of perspective. Henceforth, the simplicity of Christ is our model mindset. Rendering existence into a passage to eternal life, desire accordingly strives along a way now no longer paved by the temporal projects that we wish to pursue, but rather by way of a new way, the way beginning with accepting the task that seeks as its end something nowhere here on earth, but eternal life only.

Thus, the incarnation reorders time, and with it the life of whoever lives in light of it. Through the assuming of a human body and our fundamental condition, Christ opens a way reconciling us to God, one furthermore through which, by his example, we may emulate ourselves. Transforming existence from a project we make of ourselves into a task we receive from God, life aims at an absolute resolution beyond any of the relative things consigned to time. Above all, the way of Christ overcomes the power of death, displacing it so that death now ceases to occupy the absolute status it had before. By taking on a temporal existence ending in his own death, Christ shows us how God would have us face our own death, the most fundamental of all human experiences. Death remains no less our temporal end, in that it is as compulsory as ever before, but it is not the absolute end in the sense of being an ultimate concern. What concerns us far more is the promise of eternal life that has overcome death. This is why, for example, when explaining the incarnation's majesty, the letter to the Hebrews does so in virtue of Christ's becoming a partaker of flesh and blood: "He himself likewise took part of the same: that through death he might destroy him that had the power of death, that is, the devil; And deliver them who through fear of death were all their lifetime subject to bondage" (Heb. 2:14–15). The eternal and incarnate Word defeats death. Where once death reigned, now Christ does, enthroned as the absolute horizon of time, and hence human existence.

Death's subordination to eternal life entails that mortal life be a way of striving, not of actualizing ourselves through our own possibilities, but rather of making ourselves a reflection of the eternal prototype upon which our temporal lives are patterned. The economy of desire evinces death has been overcome, for it seeks its completion in an end lying beyond any finite ends in the time leading to death. Finding this way of living freed from death will straightaway require us to leave off the way that we had been following, the way of death, the way set before us by the pursuit of mere temporal things only.

How to exit the broad way of death is the subject of Caravaggio's masterpiece. Accordingly, he stages the road to Damascus dramatically, as being a spiritual crossroads between living and death, a crisis whereby Paul is thrown into great turmoil, for everything he knows, or thought he knew, is placed into upheaval. The one who had been traveling along his own way with a destination firmly in mind, and a goal, experiences everything obliterated suddenly. At the beginning of his journey, there seemed to be a clarity of purpose. He is driven by animosity: "Breathing out threatening and slaughter against the disciples" (Acts 9:1). For Paul, the road to Damascus appears through the lens of his own goal, one for its own part determined by a misguided conception of what is best, and which leads him to aim at bringing back Christians to Jerusalem in chains. In a moment, he is blinded by a light from heaven throwing all that into question. The very meaning of his desire to reach Damascus is overturned, for he is thrust before the gaze of God high above him, and he feels it to be so. What had seemed to him on setting out to Damascus to be absolute (the value of his own desired ends) is swept away. Effecting a thoroughgoing subversion of confidence, whether Paul can even be said to be traveling to Damascus for reasons pursuant to his own genuine best interests is cast in doubt. For the original goal to which his desire had led him is revealed to be contrary to his own good. By striking out on his way for Damascus to persecute those of this other way, he was only departing from God's ways. The biblical account tells of how Paul fell to earth under the crushing realization of his error, and the power of the voice speaking to him. To accentuate this counter-experience's shock, this experience of no longer being the one in charge but being subjected to the authority of another, Caravaggio has Paul sprawled on his back, eyes closed, knees lifted, arms outstretched skyward, a horse gingerly stepping over his helmetless head. Yet Paul is not held hostage to the searching gaze of just anyone. Overwhelmed, he struggles to identify the one from above, the God who has knocked him down to the ground: "Who art thou, Lord?" (Acts 9:5).

Supplementing the narrative given in the Acts, the author of Hebrews explains that, if Paul on the road to Damascus was still blind to Christ, it was because his desires had blinded him to the way, the way of Christ. Instead of following Jesus, Paul was persecuting those who are. Just as the "fathers in the wilderness" who hardened their hearts against God (Heb. 3:8) during the forty years, so too here an "evil heart of unbelief" estranges Paul from God. Where Hebrews attributes a blindness to the will of God to a hardness of heart, this "error in the heart" (Heb. 3:11) is elsewhere referenced with the notion of a "veil," of a garment obstructing the heart's sight of God. Paul in his second letter to the Corinthians speaks of those who do not follow Christ as those who still have a "veil upon their heart" (2 Cor. 3:15). And as the surrounding context of the text in which the veil metaphor is mentioned makes clear, he is discussing unconverted Jews, those who "read Moses" yet do not see that Jesus is the Messiah. In the letter to the church at Ephesus, Paul returns to the metaphor, this time with a twist, invoking the notion of the understanding (or the heart) having eyes: "the eyes of your understanding be enlightened" (Eph. 1:18).

Enlightenment here means transformation, the renewal of the heart. More specifically, the prophet Ezekiel characterizes conversion as an event of moral renewal. It is necessary to purge the heart, to wipe the slate clean, to move past our old failings by renouncing them once and for all: "Therefore I will judge you, O house of Israel, every one according to his ways, saith the Lord God. Repent, and turn yourselves from all your transgressions; so iniquity shall not be your ruin" (Ezek. 18:30).

As the next verse states, God makes reconciliation possible through repentance, through the decision to wash away the blots on our heart: "Cast away from you all your transgressions, whereby ye have transgressed; and make you a new heart and a new spirit" (Ezek. 18:31). And it is a reconciliation uniting us to God experientially, fusing our wills together in love. Now we are of one mind!

How to understand this newfound state of concord between God and us? Paul's conversion, which opens both his eyes and ears, effects a change of heart, for, as a long tradition going back to the patristics has observed, the heart has its own senses. As dramatic as it may be, Paul's about-face is an exemplar for anyone's as well. The French philosopher Jean-Louis Chrétien's magisterial *Symbolique du corps*, a study of the Old Testament's Song of Songs, explores the idea beautifully, following a venerable line of thinkers having noted that everyone's heart has its eyes, ears, nose, mouth, and hands. And for this reason, there is a difference between what Paul calls the "outer man" and the "inward man" (2 Cor. 4:16), or the natural man and the spiritual man (1 Cor. 2:14), respectively. The latter is the one for whom the spiritual senses are active, the former the one for whom only the carnal senses are operative. Outside Damascus, Paul is blinded to the visible by the light of God, and yet, while his carnal eyes are shut for three days (Acts 9:9), his spiritual eyes are made open to God. Caravaggio captures the paradoxicality of the situation in *The Conversion of Saint Paul* (1600–01). As with the painting at the Cerasi Chapel, this vision of the Damascus scene highlights how an encounter with Christ interrupts what before it had been mundane. The version here, which its patron Monsignor Tiberio Cerasi rejected, led Caravaggio to produce the second version discussed above. This less famous original version at the Odescalchi Balbi Collection in Rome exhibits the characteristic tenebrism the Italian painter pioneered, and for which he is so well known. Its composition's figures are more tangled than in the other. While the later Cerasi Chapel painting depicts a clearly delineated Paul, horse, and horse's groom, the version presently under consideration is much more hectic. All five figures are in a flurry, Paul, a soldier, horse, an angel, and Jesus, illuminated in light, the dramatic effect of which is heightened by the pitch darkness enshrouding them from behind and on all sides. Without a trace of visible landscape to be seen, there is nothing to orient us in a shared public space. Caravaggio reduces everything on the road to the essential, to the encounter between Paul and Christ and how those immediately around them react to it. The brilliance of Christ saturates the emerging apostle, blinding his carnal eyes, but yet, rather than leaving him insensible, the encounter results in a gain, not a loss, by revealing to him an invisibility in which spiritual things reside. The Italian master shows that conversion does not only follow in response from seeing the error of continuing on our current way, for it simultaneously presents a new way by activating the very senses necessary in order to navigate it. Christ halts us along our way, and opens a wholly new way.

First of all, an encounter with God of this kind isolates us, bringing us before God without others mediating between us. Caravaggio captures the personal urgency of it well, showing how Paul, in crisis, is oblivious to the commotion around him. With God commanding Paul's attention completely, for him, others may as well not be there at all. In the moment of crisis on our life's journey, God confronts us with the choice of whether to continue on the way we have known, or whether instead to abandon those ways and strike out on a new way. When God addresses us like this, the choice of how to respond remains ours solely, and, in the moment of our choosing to convert, we hear nothing but the voice of God, certainly not the voices of those around us. The road to Damascus for Paul, consequently, presents a fork in the form of a crisis. Caravaggio shows the future apostle with his hands covering his eyes, blinded by the light. Behind him, a companion with spear drawn and shield raised tries to calm the startled horse while readying to face the unlocatable foe. Supported by an angel, Jesus reaches down his arms to Paul in a beckoning gesture. Just as Paul is blind to the frantic events unfolding on the road around him, so too he is deaf to them, the riled sounds of the spooked horse drowned out by the thundering heavenly voice. The biblical text relates it that, while everyone around Paul did see a blinding light despite "seeing no man" (Acts 9:7), they did not hear the accompanying voice of God for Paul alone. Beautifully, Caravaggio renders everything on the road around Paul into a state of indifference, and hence darkness. The light of Christ eclipses all else, but only Paul hears what the light says.

Does light speak? Or, is this simply an empty metaphor? Far from it! Not only are there spiritual senses, but, like the carnal senses, they are cross-modal, cooperating with one another to bring us into contact with what awaits to address us. At the moment of conversion, the spiritual life commences. Among other things, this means one henceforth assumes responsibility for undertaking the work God appoints one to do. And to do the work of God will require being sensitive to what he wants to tell us, so that he can guide us. To begin with, sensing what God is communicating to us will, as Paul in his letter to the Galatians notes, means working alone by oneself. For in the spirit, one bears one's own burden (Gal. 6:5). Whereas the outer man is concerned with others, and does not take responsibility for the life God is calling him to enter, a life that would require him to establish and deepen a relationship with God through his spiritual senses, the inner man labors alone before God, carrying out the task that is his alone to accomplish. What characterizes this inner life, this life of the heart attuned to God, but the heart's senses responsible for keeping us in touch with him, and so guiding us on the way to eternal life?

A philosophical tradition counting Aristotle among its

number has held that touch is the most basic, most fundamental, of the five senses. It says five, because according to this same tradition, the senses can be neatly distinguished from one another by their corresponding proper sensible, the thing to which they are suited (Aristotle would say designed) to sense. Hence, there is the sense and its sensible: vision (color), hearing (sound), smell (odor), taste (savor), and touch. And furthermore, for each sense there is its organ: eye, ear, nose, mouth, and hand. These are the five senses of the outer man, the senses of the flesh. What then of the inward man, the senses of the spirit, the epicenter of which is the heart?

First, there are the heart's eyes. They see the way. Seeing in this instance is a matter of intuition in the classical sense in which the Latin means it, *intueri* being a verb meaning to look at or regard something, to observe or give something our attention, or to regard something with admiration or wonder. On the way of eternal life, the narrow way, the heart intuits what is to be done in light of where we so find ourselves, its eyes seeing the situation for what it is, and what the situation in turn calls for. If we might compare the heart to a raft and life to the rapids, then the heart's eyes are the raft's helmsman. Spotting trouble ahead, the eyes pilot us so that we reach our destination, avoiding any calamity along the way there. To perform their task of navigation, the eyes are vigilant for what lies well beyond what is most proximate to us, and, taking the long view, they train themselves on Christ. Spiritual sight consequently involves trusting. For example, when driving a car on the curve of a highway on-ramp to enter traffic, it is best to look as far ahead as possible, and, keeping one's eye on a distant point rather than the stretch of roadway nearer to the hood, the resulting ride is smoother, the turn taken tighter. The eyes want to peek at the immediate roadway, and it takes considerable effort to keep focus on the target off in the distance. But if the eyes do so, and resist this urge to look at what is directly before us, the curve straightens, as it were, and everything falls into place without a hitch. Is it not the same with life itself? When the heart's eyes maintain their focus on God and pay less attention to whatever at the moment may seem nearer, we find our proper path, seeing the way God wants us to take, rather than the various other ways that might have led us to stray. These eyes of the heart look to the horizon, which is Christ himself. They keep us on the narrow way.

In turn, there are the ears of the heart. Whereas the eyes function primarily to handle whatever approaching matters are at a distance, by actively stretching us to see what is far from us, the ears, while likewise informing us of what surrounds us or is looming ahead, are receptive to what is close. This is not to say that they are inactive or entirely passive. To be sure, we can strain the ears of our head to hear something that is muffled or garbled, faint or too distant. The ears of our heart are in this respect no different. Sometimes, though, hearing is foremost a matter of quieting ourselves, of noticing what was always already there, closer than we had known. Here, the attention demanded to hear does not depend on straining our ears, but rather of stilling ourselves. Hearing the voice of God works in this way. The heart's ears are able to hear the words that God is speaking if we should only listen, an act of attention which requires our first silencing the ambient noise drowning it out. When we do this by opening the ears of our heart and silence what is around us, we hear what God is trying to tell us. God's voice reaches us with words instructing us of what is to be done, or what is given to understand.

Then there is the heart's mouth. If the ear listens to God's words, it is the mouth that with its own words speaks to God. Or not quite: for very often the mouth of the heart finds itself uttering God's own words in order to express itself. Often, speaking in psalms is the heart's vernacular. Our word responds to God's word, and, frequently, from the mouth will recur the very words that God himself has already spoken. God addresses us in many ways, by questioning, correcting, or encouraging us, and the mouth is able to accordingly respond, confessing, acknowledging its need of instruction, or thanking and praising. God takes the initiative through issuing the address, and if the ears respond to divine speech by listening to what is said, the mouth completes that response by offering in turn its own words to God in reply. Thus, the inward man's mouth is the instrument of prayer. For it is the mouth that voices our inner depths to God: sighing, lamenting, imploring, questioning, confiding, thanking, or praising—it utters the heart's thoughts so that God may receive its words and respond in kind. For this reason, the heart's mouth makes possible a conversation with God who is a friend, a confidante. As important as this all may be, not only does the mouth speak. For just as it speaks, so also it eats and chews. Once the ears of the heart hear, the mouth can chew on the words it has been given to consider. God's words are food to the heart. They nourish and they strengthen. And they come in a variety of tastes. Whether it be sour, as when God is seeking to correct us, or sweet, as when God is pleased with us, the heart's mouth consumes what God gives, above all the essential sustenance we need. This is why the Bible legitimately likens God's words to bread. As the heart knows that chews the "bread of life" (John 6:35), God's words are essential for the inward man, just as earthly bread is for the outer man.

Fourth, there is the nose. If it is impossible to taste without smell, so the heart cannot enjoy the presence of God without being similarly aware of evil's rot. The nose of the heart not only lets us savor the sweetness of God, but it also alerts us to any lurking evil. By repelling us from the stench of sin, the nose draws us nearer to God, and so to safety. In the Psalms, David repeatedly talks about the threat of evil coming from his many enemies seeking to destroy him. They do so by plotting and scheming, laying traps for him. Colloquially, in English, one says "I smell a trap" or that a situation or a person or an explanation "Does not pass the smell test." The nose is a suspicious organ, seeking to uncover trouble. It cooperates with the eyes, the each assisting the other to guide us on the way, preserving us from danger and keeping us from evil so that we do not stumble and fall.

Lastly, this leaves the hands. As always, it is God who takes the initiative. Stretching out his arms to grab our hand, touching our heart, God unites himself with us, ensuring that we do not lose our bearings as we walk with him along the way. When we are too tired, God lifts us up, pulling us when we could not continue on our own. When we are too scared, he leads the way, and, with a reassuring squeeze of the hand, reminds us that there is nothing to fear. The Psalms express it well, "Though I walk in the midst of trouble, thou wilt revive me: thou shalt stretch forth thine hand against the wrath of mine enemies, and thy right hand shall save me" (Psalm 138:7). The hands of the heart are not just capable of clasping onto God. For when God occasionally releases our hand, we are left to grope, to develop our hand's own skill at finding what needs to be found. The hands are free to seek and to explore. And what else would the heart's hands seek to handle but the words of life? To touch these is the spiritual hands' ultimate object, for these words are the most touching to the human heart. In his first epistle, the Apostle John notes that, by way of the incarnation, he and others have handled directly the divine. At issue is a multisensory encounter with the incarnate Word. John says, "That which was from the beginning, which we have heard, which we have seen with our eyes, which we have looked upon, and our hands have handled, of the Word of life" (1 John 1:1).

Although the spiritual senses are not perfectly interchangeable, they are mutually reinforcing. They are connected by the common tissue of grace. This economy of grace responsible for first activating and then energizing the heart's senses can be made perspicuous by its absence, the deficit of which is manifest in doubt, a subject Caravaggio explores in *The Incredulity of Saint Thomas* (1601–1602). Turning to the painting, it is worth recounting the context. Christ has been handed over to the Romans, tortured and crucified, and buried. Three days later, reports from eyewitnesses begin circulating of something miraculous: Jesus has risen from the dead! Mary Magdalene and some of the other women claim to have seen him for themselves, but their testimony is discounted by the male disciples. Later that evening on the same day, Christ appears among their midst, in the process "[showing] unto them his hands and his side" (John 20:20). Glad to see him, the disciples can hardly believe their eyes. But there is no doubting, for their friend is right here before them in the flesh. Telling them that he must return to the Father, Christ breathes on them so that they receive the Holy Ghost. The text notes, however, that Thomas, one of the twelve disciples, "was not with them when Jesus came" (John 20:23). When the other disciples tell Thomas of what has happened, he does not believe. He responds with a remark for which he has earned the moniker "Doubting Thomas," saying, "Except I shall see in his hands the mark of the nails, and put my finger into the mark of the nails, and put my hand into his side, I will not believe" (John 20:25). For Thomas, nothing short of seeing and touching will suffice for believing.

Caravaggio shows how for the doubting apostle, touching the risen Christ means being touched down to the heart of his whole being. Doubt evaporates. Faith dawns. As the gospel account relates it, Christ enters through the shut doors of the room where the disciples are gathered (the spiritual body is physical but more powerful than the merely mortal body), and immediately addresses Thomas directly: "Reach hither thy finger, and behold my hands; and reach hither thy hand, and thrust it into my side: and be not faithless, but believing" (John 20:27). Extraordinary! Words of rebuke, to be sure, but words that ultimately upbuild the one whom they address. For the very rebuke presupposes a knowledge that Jesus could possess only if he had been privy to Thomas's earlier words. Even when he was not present bodily with the disciples, he heard what Thomas said, and now he addresses Thomas, or better, his doubting heart. In reply, Thomas no longer doubts, but praises: "My Lord and my God" (John 20:28). Caravaggio exploits an indeterminateness in the text, for although John describes Thomas as saying what he does without actually touching Christ, this does not exclude the natural possibility that Thomas did indeed touch Christ after seeing him. Once again, this work, like the two paintings of Paul's conversion, is in chiaroscuro. Christ in a discolored white linen is on the left, his standing body turned to face us. With his torso exposed from the abdomen up to his left shoulder, his left hand grasps and guides Thomas's pointed finger to the pierced wound on his right side that he received from the spear while nailed on the cross. Caravaggio leaves the rest of Christ's body unmutilated, despite the fact that there would have been other heinous wounds from the flaying he had endured before being crucified. But this forensic departure from reality proves minor, for underscoring the existence of this one particular wound in fact does well to accentuate the role of prophecy. As Luke's Gospel notes, while on the road to Emmaus, Christ told the two disciples with whom he walked that the Scriptures spoke of him. One clear example of such a case is in Psalm twenty-two, where David foretells of Christ's suffering on the cross: "My strength is dried up like a potsherd; and my tongue cleaveth to my jaws; and thou hast brought me into the dust of death. For dogs have compassed me: the assembly of the wicked have inclosed me: they have pierced my hands and my feet. I may tell all my bones: they look and stare upon me. They part my garments among them, and cast lost upon my vesture" (Psalm 22:15–18). Christ, it turns out, withstood the taunts and provocations of his persecutors on the cross so that he could fulfill the words prophesied about him in the Old Testament, words that once fulfilled would allay the doubt of his followers such as Thomas. What seemed to be weakness proves to have been power, for by laying down his life on the cross and allowing sinners to have their way with him, Christ overcomes death by fulfilling the Scriptures, thereby demonstrating he is the very one his detractors had claimed he was not. Thomas is shown staring into the wound, two disciples with him looking on with similar intent. This is not the autopsy of a dead man, an item of forensic or morbid curiosity. In this transformative encounter with a man raised from the dead, it is the Living One who, in *propria persona*, overturns everything concerning what we had formerly thought about the mortal body and life.

As Paul notes of the transformation at stake, the body itself is no longer handed over to death, but now belongs to eternal life. This radical transfiguration entails a change in how we understand and in turn experience our embodiment. The body is not simply ours, the means by which we act and move in the world, with an eye to satisfying our desires or accomplishing our goals. That was the way of death, the way underwritten by "an evil heart of unbelief" (Heb. 3:12) that had failed to see its own bodily condition in light of the law of God, and had substituted its own lusts for the law. Reproving the evil of this way, Christ shows the body's true way, that it is to be a righteous body, an instrument for good, a power for carrying out the will of God. Unlike the purely carnal body that has no law above what it desires, the body given over to the pursuit of fleeting things, the body handed over to death, the body that is not yet operated by the heart open to God, the spiritual body, in contrast, is the body that has died to its lusts, and, "walking in newness of life" (Rom. 6:4) consecrates itself to life, not the life of gratifying its lustful desires, but of eternal life, the life that attuned to God seeks after eternal things. The body of the believer enacts what Paul and Thomas learned through their respective encounters with the Word: "the wages of sin is death, [but] the gift of God is eternal life in Christ Jesus" (Rom. 6:23). This is what Paul says two chapters later in the same epistle. Drawing again a distinction between the flesh and the spirit, he notes it is the body of the believer which, yielding to God rather than to sin, fulfills the law of righteousness by submitting to the ways of the Holy Spirit, in short, the way of those "who walk not after flesh but after the Spirit" (Rom. 8:1). For the mortal life that lives in expectation of the promise of mortal life, the body itself points to the resurrection, to the glory to come: "For which cause we faint not but though our outward man perish, yet the inward man is renewed day by day. For our light affliction, which is but for a moment, worketh for us a far more exceeding and eternal weight of glory: While we look not at the things which are seen, but at the things which are not seen: for the things which are seen are temporal, but the things which are not seen are eternal" (2 Cor. 4:16–18). With the incarnation, Christ accordingly has opened "a new and living way" (Heb. 10:20), the new covenant Deuteronomy spoke of at last being instituted through the veil of his flesh, a covenant whose union between God and us is accomplished at the heart of our being, this living way having touched us, alerting us to the fact that the way we had known before, the way of death, is superseded, the way of eternal life now a way we see, hear, taste, smell, and touch.

Paul, as Saul, set out on the road to Damascus intent on binding those following the way. When on this way, his way, he encountered Christ, and realized it was actually he, Saul, who was bound. Chained and blinded by his wayward desire! All of us at some point have our Damascus. How we respond to the mercy is up to us, whether to continue on according to our own ways, or, at last, to follow the Way.

Chapter 6

The Purple Robe

For a long time, we experience the call of God despite our unwillingness to listen, for the fear of man dissuades us. We feel the weight upon us of the claim to begin another life, one we know we have not yet begun, because afraid, we turn away in the face of the suffering that will accompany our rebirth, and so we procrastinate, putting off the decision to commence on the life we know would be ours to endure, the life that would allow us to be ourselves, rather than the current one we have chosen for whatever the reason. Try as we do to avoid it, events remind us how true independence without freedom in Christ is impossible, a freedom, in turn, that can come to fruition only by incessantly dispossessing ourselves of anything that hinders God's activity in our lives, the primary obstacle of which, initially at least, is our reluctance to repent owing to the fear of the persecution we know would follow. To be free, it will be necessary to suffer, and there is no way around it. And so, beginning anew takes trust. Later, when we have done so, and find ourselves embarked on a life in Christ that is ours, we see how our fears had been misplaced, for we had failed to fathom the full extent of God's faithfulness. Difficult as what comes may be, we are never left to face it alone. Contrary to the misunderstanding which for a while had stopped us from converting, to follow the way God appoints is not to be asked to endure anything more than we can bear, as God is with us always.

When, hence, the suffering along this new way would be enough to make us faint, the persecution being too great, an angel of the Lord comes to us bearing a message. The angel speaks, "They hate you for your heart." The message delivered tells us what we already know, yet no less had to hear. God breathes on us, consoles us and restores us, by making everything feel clean. Like a gust of wind, its truth disperses all the confusion: slander vanishes, taunting ceases, as at last we experience a respite, for evil recedes. God's words to us evaporate the dark cloud, and the sun shines again. In these encounters capable of rendering everything ephemeral, including our sufferings, the burden lifts. Lucid states like these lift us up, humidifying us into the clear air of grace, making us tremble at the expectation of one day entering the glory of God's kingdom, and so, seeing our task, reminded of our vocation to press on, we do what must be done today, affirming God's call to face the hatred we encounter as a blessing. Providence passes through human suffering, each of us in our way serving as little agents of destiny, of God's will. The angel reminds us of it, counseling us never to forget nothing is more wonderful than to suffer undeservedly for doing what is called of us.

In his Sermon on the Mount, such is the message Christ gives to the multitude assembled to hear him, when in the Beatitudes he speaks of all of life's blessings, including the apparently counterintuitive one of being persecuted. As Luke's Gospel says, "Blessed are ye, when men shall hate you, and when they shall separate you from their company, and shall reproach you, and cast out your name as evil, for the Son of man's sake" (Luke 6:22). To suffer in *this* way is to be hated for choosing to walk in Christ's footsteps, to be rejected, scorned, and opposed, for deciding to follow the way of righteousness rather than evil. He explains how this persecution is to be understood, that accordingly it be identified correctly for the blessing it is. Suffering's iridescence leaves it open to interpretation. How are we to respond? According to Christ, nothing less than rejoicing is appropriate. Directly reversing the commonplace that equates suffering with undesirableness, we read the opposite in Matthew's account, where it is said, "Blessed are they which are persecuted for righteousness' sake: for theirs is the kingdom of heaven. Blessed are ye, when men shall revile you, and persecute you, and shall say all manner of evil against you falsely for my sake. Rejoice, and be exceedingly glad: for great is your reward in heaven: for so persecuted they the prophets which were before you" (Matt. 5:10–12). To be sure, certain everyday adages encourage those who live by them to discount such suffering — "That's how the world is," "Life is hard," or simply "Life is not fair." These trite sayings roll off the tongues of those who do not know the first thing about the spiritual trial they so cavalierly ignore. How, indeed, could those who say these things possibly know? The secret of suffering is not yet revealed to them, but rather to those who follow the way of the most unjustly hated, most wrongly persecuted, man to ever walk the earth. Follow Jesus Christ, then one learns what suffering is! Follow Christ, and then, like him, one will see one's sufferings brushed aside exasperatedly by those who, absorbed entirely with existing for nothing higher than themselves, avoid the suffering they know awaits them too, were they also to begin seeking the kingdom of heaven.

As a consequence of his denying Christ, Peter learned clearly that it is not possible to have Christ while evading his sufferings. Having learned his lesson, he in an epistle to fellow believers addresses the worry that all of the newly converted must confront, when everything they thought they possessed and everything they thought they knew is suddenly thrown into upheaval. When Christ becomes the rock, all else, however solid, gives way. Old friends resent and abandon us. Family members attack us. Acquaintances avoid us. And as for those already who consider us their enemies, they delight in it all! In the face of the strife, it is imperative not to quit, not to think something has gone terribly awry, but to accept such challenges are inevitable, and thus to take them as the matter of course they in fact are. Likening the adversity to a firestorm, Peter says, "Think it not strange concerning the fiery trial which is to try you, as though some strange thing happened unto you: But rejoice, inasmuch as ye are partakers of Christ's sufferings" (1 Pet. 4:13). Not only is the trial to be endured, it is to be embraced, welcomed with open arms as a sign that one is on the path to salvation, a path set by way of a sanctification itself accomplishable only in the response to suffering. Peter's suggestion concerning the fiery trial conversion ignites is to hold fast in the midst of suffering, understanding that it is expected. As he explains it, here steadfastness amid tribulation means continuing on the way leading to eternal life, by accepting being hated for following Christ. For as Peter states next, the one above all whom those hating us hate is really Christ, the object of their hatred for having exposed their sin: "If ye be reproached for the name of Christ, happy are ye; for the spirit of glory and of God resteth upon you: on their part he is evil spoken of, but on your part he is glorified" (1 Pet. 4:14–15). In the wake of conversion, obviously the typical praise and honor from others are out the window. Instead, it is now slander, insults, and whisperings. Peter's own advice for how we are to react eclipses mere psychological counseling and its correspondingly banal suggestion to try to keep a positive attitude. His remark is insightful, for it addresses an experiential fact, a fact grounded in a spiritual necessity concerning how things must be, if one is to be willing to enter the kingdom of heaven. In life, those esteeming the approval of others will never discover the path to eternal life, for, as Christ underscores, the way to eternal life necessitates no longer seeking such approval, but instead only the approval coming from God: "How can ye believe, which receive honour one of another, and seek not the honour that cometh from God only?" (John 5:44).

First of all with Christ, then for anyone who ponders the decision of whether or not to commit to following him, the crucible starts with facing what the Scriptures call the "fear of man." Overcoming the fear at stake requires accepting that doing so will entail becoming increasingly isolated. This was true in Christ's own case, for he was rejected by essentially everyone: disbelieved by his brothers and sisters, betrayed by Judas, denied by Peter, left to endure his suffering alone in Gethsemane, and forsaken to die mocked on the cross. When resisting the fear of man triggers a chain of events involving consequences as severe as these, it is understandable why it takes courage to begin. From the perspective of someone still living under the tyranny of seeking the approval of others, the danger may appear to consist in confronting the fear itself, for it is confronting it that invites persecution and all of the suffering that otherwise could be avoided. Here worldly prudence strongly recommends cowardice, it would seem. And yet, a passage in the Proverbs turns this apparent wisdom on its head, highlighting instead how the real danger is indulging the fear of man. For such fear "lays a snare" (Prov 29:25). The truly fearful thing is failing to be rid of the fear, for it leaves us imprisoned to others, unable to discern the will of God, and thus unfit to enter his kingdom. At issue is a reversal of the self-interested logic of what the world considers common sense, what Paul calls the world's wisdom. All else being equal, naturally we prefer to be liked by others. Nobody enjoys being disliked unfairly, and certainly nobody enjoys being disliked purely for the sake of being disliked. Sometimes, it is true, we might not despair for being disliked, if we believe the negative judgments of others are misplaced, either because they have bad motives in forming them, or are otherwise being unfair. Being on the receiving end of disapproval from others need not be entirely bad. Even so, the fear of being disliked, criticized, or ostracized, exerts a powerful hold. We fear the insults of others. We fear incurring their disappointment. We fear being shunned, fear upsetting those on whom we have come to depend. For anyone who has not yet been liberated from the fear of living without the approval of others knows, others are seen to validate and assure us, an approval we cannot imagine existing without, for in its absence, our identity depending upon it would be incinerated, blown away by the winds like a puff of smoke. While the fear of man involves a preoccupation with others, it is at bottom self-regarding, for its concern with keeping others happy is fed by wanting to preserve what it sees as beneficial to itself, whether that be reputation and standing, influence and power, or plain and simple comfort. So long as we are unprepared to die to others, it is because we hesitate to change, unwilling to live without the innumerable things to which we cling.

In what regard does surpassing the fear of man take dying to others? A call to authenticity is not at issue. Spiritually speaking, dying to others does not involve embarking on the pursuit for originality or eccentricity. Nor for that matter does it entail selfishness, much less license it. The paradox of authenticity is that, in seeking to differentiate itself from others, in doing so it concerns itself with whether others recognize that difference. For authenticity, others remain the measure. Inherently, it is social, for the very goal of being unique or original presupposes a concern with others, with differentiating oneself from them. For this reason, authenticity is incapable of overcoming the fear of man's greatest fear of all, of becoming dead to those we know, scorned, mocked, and misunderstood. Dying, here, takes a readiness to learn to live alone, not in the sight of others, however, but as an individual before God only, somebody no longer seeking to receive the approval of the crowd. The task is not fundamentally negative, not defined by the desire to subvert what is customary or typical simply for the sake of being different. The contrarian is as concerned with others as the conformist. This is different. Instead, whatever difference between others and oneself emerges is the consequence of focusing on an independent positive measure: the will of God. If one happens to become original or unique as a consequence, it comes about from having first conformed oneself to the will of God, and not for its own sake. Hence, breaking free from the opinion of others is not equivalent to authenticity's quest, and is not the existence of the nonconformist or the contrarian intent on leaving a recognizable mark in this world. It is, rather, the journey of the pilgrim. Instead of meeting the expectations of others, the goal is meeting God's expectations. God's approval is what matters, and thus our actions are undertaken, not with an eye to showing others that we are different than they, but with the sole aim of proving our sincerity to God. Action is not about being seen by others, but being honest with God. When resolving to fear God rather than others, the task of becoming the individual God wants us to be subordinates the project of becoming what others think we should be.

Deciding to be ourselves before God changes our relations to others. Frequently, the fallout begins with family. When Christ says that he has come to earth with "a sword" (Matthew 10:34), he means he has come to sever established allegiances. By laying down the rule that we are to love God more than we love even ourselves, Christ seeks to short-circuit everyday life's regime of self-interest. Relations are to be premised on what God expects of us, not what we think would be in our own personal interest. Before seeing ourselves as part of a group or clan, we are to see ourselves as individuals before God. This means family is no longer first. Christ states explicitly that anyone who loves his kin more than God will not find God, for, "He that loveth father or mother more than me is not worthy of me: and he that loveth son or daughter more than me is not worthy of me" (Matt. 10:37). If conversion's strain on family relations is not already bad, then there are friends. In short order, we come to find many of those we had thought were friends actually are not. Once again, Peter explicates the process by which we come to depend on God, when we realize that we can no longer depend on those we once believed were friends. He says,

"Forasmuch then as Christ hath suffered for us in the flesh, arm yourselves likewise with the same mind [....] That he no longer should live the rest of his time in the flesh to the lusts of men, but to the will of God. For the time past of our life may suffice us to have wrought the will of the Gentiles, when we walked in lasciviousness, lusts, excess of wine, revellings, banquetings, and abominable idolatries: Wherein they think it strange that ye run not with them to the same excess of riot, speaking evil of you: Who shall give account to him that is ready to judge the quick and the dead" (1 Pet. 4:1–5). Whereas we were previously controlled by how others might respond to us, now we are free from fear, only concerned with how God sees us. True identity lies in Christ, not the opinion of others.

Why does coming to Christ provoke consternation in those who have not yet done so for themselves? To borrow Christ's language, why does converting cause offense? Somebody's conversion is a reminder to everyone else that the world is in rebellion to God. In bad faith, evil tries to conceal this rebellion. As Kierkegaard put it, converting is accordingly "treason to the world." It is treason in the eyes of others, because in deciding to serve God, one testifies that one no longer desires to oppose God, and hence that others are in effect opposing God by not doing the same. To submit to God is to remind others they too are called to do so.

The simmering rebellion in turn boils over. Due to the predictability of the twisted logic according to which evil unfolds, the progressively vehement stages of its hatred for the truth can be adduced *a priori*. A sketch of its progression will suffice. Consider evil, and it is clear why it gives rise to persecution. Evil hates innocence, despises what is pure. Evil is scornful, loathing of anything embodying the good that it hates itself for disavowing. Whatever serves as a reminder of its own deformity must be ignored, and if it cannot be ignored, deprecated. And in its fury to tear down anything (but especially anyone) calling to mind the decision it has made to betray the good, evil relishes tormenting what it resents, particularly those over whom it most of all seeks to establish its power, that is to say, those who oppose it, by remaining faithful to the light, and so to God. Evil renounces doing the good, the consequence of which is a guilt compelling it to compensate by striving for control, for domination, and hence, above all, by struggling against the truth, for the truth threatens evil's monomaniacal desire to be in charge, to subjugate everything under itself, to eliminate the least trace of its dislike of itself. In short, because evil already hates itself, it hates the truth with it, for truth is the mirror in which evil is forced to see its ugliness for what it is.

Attacking this sickness at its roots, truth subverts evil's systems of deceit, its coordinated and interlocking tissue of lies without which it would not survive, much less thrive. This earns truth evil's ire. Several things can be noted about the ensuing rage. To begin with, it must be said that, contrary to all of evil's own blustering, it simply spews forth from weakness, which is why, in a pinch, it always resorts to hiding behind lies and other deceits. Of course, in doing so, evil flatters itself falsely. For although it is correct in its belief that deceiving takes cunning, such cunningness is exercised only as a result of evil's inability to be direct, and its powerlessness to show itself for what it is. Ultimately, then, evil is not so powerful at all. As a consequence, by necessity, lying is evil's main defense, for in its weakness, evil acknowledges itself to be unable to salvage its plans except by deploying its purported strength in the form of dishonesty, deflection, or some other kind of smokescreen. Thus, to cut evil down to size and to dispel its unwarranted popular mystique, asking one simple question suffices to dispense with all its vain pretensions to power: if evil is so strong, why must it hide, deflect, and deceive? And as for the good at which it scoffs, by contrast, it is natural and direct. This simple plainness explains why the good is strong, so strong, in fact, that in the last analysis goodness is impervious to any of evil's lies. Eventually, all lies yield to the truth. The evil one, invariably, falls silent.

When truth corners evil by exposing evil for what it has done, is it surprising that evil slinks away into a dark silence, only to later, as so often happens, after gathering itself for a response, lash out in violence, even sometimes resorting to the desperate extreme of committing murder? What fuels this evil writhing in brooding silence, this evil seething with infernal rage, this evil festering in hatred, triggered to violence by anyone it deems to have impudently challenged it? In its darkened understanding, what are this evil mind's twisted reasons, its contorted logic? What peculiar sort of compulsion drives it, conjuring its words and governing its deeds? What warped rationale leads it to countenance only two options when it knows it has been exposed for everybody to see: in short, either to cower in silence or else to wield violence? Why does evil follow the recurring pattern it does: first, attempts to establish plausible deniability; next, vehement denials when those initial attempts fail; then a silence thick with guilt; and finally, when it dares to resurface after being exposed, violence.

Pride is at work at every stage. Pride fuels the self-seeking desire to which it gives rise, a desire so intoxicated with perceived grandeur that it coronates itself king, and thus feels itself to be entitled to lie, to slander, even to kill. Evil, here, takes the form of a kingdom of self. It is a despotic kingdom, and not by accident. For everything about this kind of evil stems from its tyrannical impulse to get its own way, no matter the harm doing so causes others, or even itself. No obstacle can be allowed to impede it, no force to thwart it, and certainly not the truth of all things—truth, evil's sworn enemy, greatest hinderance, most abiding inconvenience, that which above all defies it. No, never! The truth must not prevail! For such evil, the desire to block the truth from receiving the standing it deserves becomes an obsession, what it takes to be a duty. Its efforts to do so are transparently self-serving. Evil attacks the truth, because the truth brings to light the good. To destroy the good, evil finds it necessary to suppress the truth. But a truth made manifest cannot be refuted by lies. And for this reason, lies are evil's penultimate defense. But only penultimate. For although evil might rarely state the fact, it always keeps in mind a "fail safe" — violence.

Hence, when deception and deflection have run their course to no avail, evil's stand against the good shifts ground. Jettisoning any appearance to care about logic, evidence, or reason, and knowing that the truth stands to be neutralized only by some entirely other means, here a dark thought takes shape in its mind: "Perhaps it will be necessary to kill... Yes, that would make things much easier, would solve the problem!" When the truth no longer can be ignored but must be addressed, best of all, so evil decides, to kill whoever speaks the very truth itself that it cannot eliminate. Evil kills the messenger of the truth, the one who delivers the truth evil knows itself to be unable to conceal, discredit, or destroy. The coerciveness of its inner logic at last fully divulged, evil is shown to have been founded on a lie, for, unable to win others to its side by example or persuasion (its purported truth now unmasked as an obvious lie), it resorts to other means. Intimidation, threats of violence, and, when necessary in its view, actual violence.

How must the good respond? Here, the stakes intensify. Fear of man no longer entails becoming dead to others, in that one might be the recipient of their disapproval or criticism. Now there is the possibility of being attacked, even killed. Dying to others means being prepared to have them literally put one to death. Far worse than simply receiving the scorn of others rather than their praise or honor, now hatred turns murderous. It is no longer sufficient to destroy us in a verbal effigy, slandering or mocking a pinata to bash. Beyond the bitter words from "the swords of tongues," violence is directed at us in the flesh directly. At this point, facing the fear of man means facing the fear of death. To do so in a way that will preserve our integrity, it will be necessary to fear God. As Christ says, "And do not fear those who kill the body but cannot kill the soul. Rather fear him who can destroy both soul and body in hell" (Matt. 10:28).

Over the years, many masters such as Rubens and Rembrandt have made the Passion their subject. What is done to Christ exhibits the true face of evil, all its sordid and sadistic tactics. And in a world populated by the evil sketched above, is it not a *fait accompli* Christ, who spoke the truth, to be sure, but more importantly, identified himself as being the very truth itself, would be killed? As the truth incarnate, he embodies everything evil hates. From the beginning of his life, then, Christ must have understood he would be rejected by those he knew, and that his fate was to be put to a cruel and unjust death. Naturally, neither would it be enough for those who sought to kill him to do so, for they would first ensure that he should suffer in every humanly imaginable way. Looking to how Christ faced his own persecution, then, strengthens us to face the fear of man.

In the Psalms, David characterizes the one persecuting him as the "violent man" or, in a group, "bloody men" (Psalm 59:2). The evildoer is he who sheds innocent blood. Peter Paul Rubens highlights the sadism of it all in the *Flagellation of Christ*, a work completed sometime during the first-half of the seventeenth century at St Paul's Church in Antwerp, and preceded by a famous sketch of the same name. At the center stands Christ. Stripped to a linen cloth, his wrists bound in chains to a post, his exposed back streaked with blood from the whipping he is receiving, he looks at the ground. True to the style for which his figures are known, Rubens depicts Christ as powerful and muscular. This is not the traditional emaciated, weak figure of Christ so common to the genre. Nonetheless, he is demur, reticent and resigned to his suffering, apparently at peace with the fact that he is in the hands of bestial men who are enjoying flagellating him. As for these others, they are crowded around him, the one soldier with a whip standing to Christ's left, four others immediately to the right. The whipper stares fixedly at his target's back, winding up to strike. One of the other men watches with glee, a sick smile on his face, as he peers over Christ's shoulders to look on at the bloodshed. Another man, with eyes bugging out, looks entranced by the spectacle, a demonic power overtaking him. The soldier nearest the right foreground can only be seen partially, his leg kicking Christ, his arms raised above his head as he prepares to deliver a blow. In a symbol of the men's animal fury and rabid cruelty, Rubens places in their midst a menacing dog ready to bite the bound Savior. The choice of a dog is an allusion, perhaps, to a common metaphor in the Psalms for evil men, for David calls his persecutors "wicked transgressors," those for whom "swords are their lips," and who make "a noise like a dog" (Psalm 59:6). Cruel to the point of bestiality, they are mindless, and so they resort to dumb violence.

Such evil's stupidity is underscored by the nineteenth-century work by Antonio Ciseri, *Ecce Homo* (1891). The inane cruelty of Christ's being brought before the people is that they are totally incapable of judging rightly. Stirred up by the Pharisees into madness, the crowd rebuffs Pilate's attempts to get it to come to its senses. Questioning the people as to what wrong Christ has done proves fruitless—the crowd does not care that it cannot credibly accuse him of any wrongdoing. And as for Pilate's asking the crowd what punishment Christ deserves for his purported crimes, it only invites worse madness: "Crucify him! Crucify him!" (Luke 23:21). It is not enough to ridicule and scourge him, no, he must be killed, put to death as a criminal worthy of execution. Ciseri places Christ in the middle, his back to the viewer, as he looks between two massive columns onto the crowd below. Pilate stands in front of him, his left arm outstretched as he presents the wounded Christ: "Behold, the man!" (John 19:5). In the work's near foreground, two women, one of whom is likely Pilate's wife, hold each other, distressed at the injustice of the situation. Christ stands in a red robe, a crown of thorns on his head, with Pilate's golden throne sitting in the court, a reminder that, although Christ is a king, his is a kingdom not of this world. Across the square is a prominent white stone building, its terraces lined with onlookers keen to see the proceedings unfold. Above everyone is a giant crystal blue sky. Everything about the scene is unnervingly expansive, haunted by an over-powering anonymity, a mood Ciseri accentuates by depicting Pilate's judgment hall from the perspective of one looking upwards from the floor of it. One figure, some Roman courtier off to the far right, and then another, a soldier on the left immediately next to Christ, both stare in the direction of the crowd with raised chins, their gazes fixed on the crowd below, but also, for reasons that are unclear, also on the sky above. Their attention is strangely divided, their focus torn between mysterious forces. The entire effect of Ciseri's piece is that nobody—neither the crowd, nor Pilate and his men—is fully in control. Something high above men is at work.

Rembrandt's version, the 1634 raw umber etching *Christ before Pilate (Ecce Homo)*, focuses keenly on the situation's competing power relations. Whereas Ciseri's work had merely implied the presence of the Pharisees, Rembrandt instead showcases their hand in things front and center. A blotted crowd on the right, the primary action lies on the work's left, with Pilate sitting in judgment, motioning to a group of Pharisees crowding up against him, their contorted faces and intruding arms revealing the desperation with which they are willing to see their plan to completion. Pilate finds himself thrown in the middle of three colliding groups all literally at his lap: his own soldiers (two of whom hold the captive Christ) looking for him to control the situation and exercise Roman authority over Judea, the restless Pharisees at his feet intent on twisting his arm into action, and, of course, the unruly and menacing crowd teeming with zealots. The only individual other than Pilate not subsumed into such a faction is Christ, who for his own part gazes off into the distance, his stare drifting above Pilate and the Pharisees, as if he has something entirely else on his mind besides the events unfolding right before him. Rembrandt shows Christ with the crown of thorns, indicating that he has already been scourged and mocked by the Roman soldiers. However, the artist decides not to show any visible signs of the torture—no lacerations, no blood. Somehow the agony is still no less apparent. Christ's face shows a deep fatigue, a readiness to get on with it, as he knows there is no possibility of reason prevailing here. This moment— his greatest agony—is one for which the Pharisees have been waiting, and the culmination of their incessant plotting and scheming. After having now twice examined Christ and finding no fault with him, certainly no fault "deserving of death" (Luke 23:15), Pilate has come to see the accused one before him is the victim of the Pharisees' envy. Rationalizing the situation, the Roman governor washes his hands, and gives Christ's persecutors what they want. Whereas Rubens had shown the situation's madness and stupidity by accentuating the Roman soldiers' bestial violence, here Rembrandt underscores Christ's predicament by highlighting the Pharisees' ghoulishness, giving them especially twisted faces, demonic expressions of which only those responsible for handing Christ over to die a death he does not deserve are capable. As all of these paintings of the Passion show, if Christ is the perfect man, the *logos* incarnate, then as for his sham trial, it is inhuman, cruel and unjust beyond words.

But it is *Christ at the Column*, Pieter Fransz de Grebber's sublime 1632 work, that perhaps best captures the injustice of the situation. Eliminating everything else to leave only the solitary figure of Christ, Grebber's work distills the state of affairs to its essence. Despite the apparent complexity of the cultural, political, and religious circumstances in Judea with all the competing interests and warring political and religious factions, things are very simple. While the Romans and the Pharisees think they have authority and vie for power, in fact they do not. Christ alone has the power. Thus, as the men around him negotiate frantically over what is to be done, he remains silent, knowing the death to which he will soon be condemned is one over which he retains the power. Nobody takes from him his life, unless it is permitted: "No man taketh it from me, but I lay it down of myself. I have power to lay it down, and I have power to take it again. This commandment have I received of my Father" (John 10:18). On multiple occasions before, his persecutors' attempts to destroy him were of no avail. John describes how at the feast of Tabernacles, for instance, Christ's brothers, who do not believe he is the Messiah, tell him to show himself openly to the world at the feast, so that everybody else may judge for themselves as to whether he is who he claims. Knowing that doing so in the way they suggest will mean being taken by the Pharisees, in reply, Christ says, "My time is not yet come: but your time is always ready" (John 7:6). He instructs them to go to the feast, while he lingers behind, for, as he says again, "my time is not yet full come" (John 7:8). Later, when he enters the temple, he challenges the Pharisees directly, answering their questions in a way demonstrating their hypocrisy and ignorance. They attempt to seize him but fail: "Then they sought to take him: but no man laid hands on him, because his hour was not yet come" (John 7:30). It is not until the feast of the Passover that his hour finally comes, and when it does, it remains a moment by which Christ might glorify the Father in heaven (John 17:1). From first to last, it is God in control, not men.

Grebber's Christ stands alone against a dark charcoal background bereft of any identifiable feature. What a gentle solemnity! Arms crossed at the wrists resting gingerly on his left hip, his left leg put slightly forward in front of his right leg, his head tilted toward his left shoulder, his eyes closed, Christ's whole body is effaced to the point of ephemerality. A black robe blending with the wall behind it drapes to the floor, his pristine white loins unblemished by the blood splatters dotting his lower abdomen. Across his forehead runs a ring of blood beneath the crown of thorns. Grebber's Christ is not nearly as muscular as Rubens' figure, but neither is he frail. His ordinary body, nonetheless, is infused with power, the very "strength in weakness" of which Paul speaks in his letters to the Corinthians, a force from above whose presence Grebber signifies with a luminous halo enshrouding Christ's head. The halo acts like a portal to a different realm, a kingdom of light, the invisible kingdom to which Christ refers when he tells Pilate that he is indeed a king. In short, this is a paradoxical power, a strength in weakness, and one to which we are all called to emulate: "And he said unto me, My grace is sufficient for thee: for my strength is made perfect in weakness. Most gladly therefore will I rather glory in my infirmities, that the power of Christ may rest upon me. Therefore I take pleasure in infirmities, in reproaches, in necessities, in persecutions, in distresses for Christ's sake: for when I am weak, then am I strong" (2 Cor. 12:9–10). It is with this juxtaposition between worldly and heavenly wisdoms in mind that the solitary Christ takes on deeper significance. Housed at the Legion of Honor in San Francisco, Grebber's unassuming piece is a study in honor, not of the temporal kind those engaged in worldly struggles for power and prestige seek, but eternal honor, the sort that comes from God only.

While Christ dies misunderstood and alone, certainly without worldly honor, it is a death accomplished in love, a sacrifice made in order to draw for all time anyone who will respond accordingly, and follow him. Thus, the Passion points to our own. Imitating Christ leads one to be hated as he was. Shortly before his arrest, Christ tells his disciples what to expect, if they should continue to follow him. His parting instructions to the disciples remind us, as it did them, that the way will not be easy. For in following him, one chooses to meet the same hatred. It will be crucial never to lose sight of the one to whom such hatred is really directed: "The world cannot hate you; but me it hateth, because I testify of it, that the works thereof are evil" (John 7:7). Betrayed by Judas, abandoned by the other disciples, Christ faces his arrest, torture, and death alone. He does so in order to pave a living way, a way through evil and beyond death. As the Book of Hebrews says, "For it became him, for whom are all things, and by whom are all things, in bringing many sons unto glory, to make the captain of their salvation perfect through sufferings" (Heb. 2:10). Christ is the exemplar, the one to whom we may look when facing our own suffering: "Looking unto Jesus the author and finisher of our faith; who for the joy that was set before him endured the cross, despising the shame, and is set down at the right hand of the throne of God. For consider him that endured such contradiction of sinners against himself, lest ye be wearied and faint in your minds" (Heb. 2:2–3). In the fifteenth chapter of John, Christ says, "If the world hates you, ye know that it hated me before it hated you" (John 15:18). To be hated by the world is to be hated for no longer belonging to it, but to God: "If ye were of the world, the world would love its own: but because ye are not of the world, but I have chosen you out of the world, therefore the world hates you" (John 15:19). It is a hatred leading to persecution: "If they persecuted me, they will also persecute you" (John 15:20). Angry with themselves over their own evil, they project hatred onto those who have been redeemed from it. Above all, this self-hatred means hating the Redeemer: "If I had not come and spoken unto them, they had not had sin: but now they have no cloak for their sin" (John 15:22). With Christ's mission fulfilled, there is no longer any excuse to remain in darkness. Everything is manifest in the light: "If I had not done among them the works which none other man did, they had not had sin: but now have they both seen and hated both me and my Father. But this cometh to pass, that the word might be fulfilled that is written in their law, They hated me without a cause" (John 15:24–25). Henceforth, there is a choice to be made, whether to be of the world and to live for others, or whether to be of God and die to them: "They are not of the world, even as I am not of the world" (John 17:16). Loved by God and thus free even to die, one lives truly, no longer burdened by worries over how others view us. No longer a prisoner to their opinion, we are free in Christ.

In the Septuagint, purple is associated with royalty, distinguished from what is common: "From him that weareth purple and a crown, unto him that is clothed with a linen frock" (Ecclus. XL.4). When Christ dons his crown of thorns, and puts on his purple robe, he accomplishes his task, subverting the wisdom of the world, thereby demonstrating his heavenly power, even when those among him take themselves to be in control. They do not hold the power of life and death, and they certainly do not hold the power to judge in eternity. In a letter to Timothy, Paul warns that everyone who heeds the way of the cross and decides to live before God will be persecuted for it: "Yea, and all that will live godly in Christ Jesus shall suffer persecution" (1 Tim. 3:12). Imprisoned for his faith, to the church at Philippi, Paul writes, "For unto you it is given in the behalf of Christ, not only to believe on him, but also to suffer for his sake" (Phil. 1:29). But there is no reason to despair. Rather, it is reason to rejoice. For as Paul explains elsewhere, life is an examination, a trial meant to prepare us for the kingdom of heaven, where we will reign in glory with Christ: "Persecuted, but not forsaken; cast down, but not destroyed; Always bearing about in the body the dying of the Lord Jesus, that the life also of Jesus might be made manifest in our body" (2 Cor. 4:9). Suffering is fleeting in the book of eternity: "For our light affliction, which is but for a moment, worketh for us a far more exceeding and eternal weight of glory" (2 Cor. 4:17). If history still remembers individuals such as Pilate and Caiaphas and Judas, it is only because of the One who was always already in charge, the One who, despite what others said of and did to him, overcame everything, death included, demonstrating his rightful claim to be "King of the Jews" (John 19:3).

Displaying the futility of evil's will to destroy the truth, Christ's personal victory over death takes on universal significance. Having passed through suffering unto death, and back to life, his resurrection guarantees the good's ultimate triumph over evil. Even when evil seemingly has overpowered the truth to the point of putting it to death, it fails, for the truth only rises again. This is the eternal power of the good originating beyond the world, a good having issued its first word with creation, and its last word with the resurrection. The chains of darkness broken, anyone who is willing to be reconciled to God may now say, "You have redeemed me, O Lord of truth" (Psalm 31:5). So much for evil, and all its little lies! The truth is risen. And on resurrection day, so too shall we be.

Chapter 7

Apparitions of the Kingdom

On the first day of creation, the Spirit of God hovered over the waters. On the day that God makes of us a new creation, the day in which we ourselves are made anew in Christ, the waters of eternal life well up from within a depth so deep in us we had not even fathomed its existence, and so then we now float, suspended atop the currents of divine grace buoying us on, like a boat gliding along a gentle surface, the breakers behind us, the tides incessantly guiding us outward on our voyage into a capacious sea. Venturing further from the sandy shores of what had once seemed normal, out beyond what had been the bounds of the habitable, increasingly we take our bearings no longer from the world, but from what instead has become the horizon of all horizons, the kingdom of heaven. Our transit is an exodus from the dry land of despair. As the marvelous Johannine theme says, "Let your joy be full" (1 John 1:4).

There is something cosmic about the transformation, a fact borne witness by the heavens and earth when they are seen brimming with this same joy. Everything sings to God. The Impressionist Alfred Sisley captures this cosmic joy in his 1877 work *The Seine at Suresnes.* Set in summer, the particular painting in question shares a title with a series of *en plein air* landscapes, which he undertook that same decade at the small commune of Suresnes nearby Paris. Unlike the other works capturing the same stretch of riverbank up close, here Sisley chooses to depict the scene otherwise, the outstretched countryside seen from ahigh a hilltop, with the river itself off in the distance. The name of this beautiful Impressionistic painting notwithstanding, it initially is not the river, but the captivating clouds above, that draw our attention, stealing the show, as it were, by ripening before us like a fruit, their glory bursting forth in the shape of big fluffy marshmellows that make us imagine what it would be like to walk on them. It is easy to see how Sisley, a French born British citizen who resided in Paris for most of his life, came to relish the open blue sky in such scarce supply in foggy London, a city that he visited for periods throughout his life, and where he came under the artistic influence of British painters such as William Turner.

As frustrating as it is to never walk on clouds, Sisley's 1877 landscape reminds us how the quotidian experience of a day in the countryside has its substantial charms all the same. The wide spectrum of emotional tonalities associated with such an experience is shown beautifully in his other Seine studies, all of which capture the intimate connection among sky, water, and the one who beholds them, by exploring the river's varying faces. The first work, done in 1874, shows the Seine in what appears to be autumn. Beginning on the left foreground is the promenade. Stretching along the river, the waterway path is almost entirely deserted, save for two blotted figures walking by a red and white boat moored in the bank's shallows. In the distance, a few scattered buildings are visible mainly due to the smoke from their chimneys. Across the river stand three trees on the other bank. Still relatively robust despite the impending winter, their sturdy terracotta and almond foliage reflects brilliantly on the face of the water. As for the river, it is shallow and tranquil, its lilac and periwinkle surface supported by an underlying supple forest green. The sky mirrors the water, the result of which is to give the entire scene a unified feeling of serenity, an achievement calling to mind what one might expect from a work of the American Tonalists.

Like the first, Sisley's second study, this one completed in 1879, accentuates the unity between sky and river. Both a soft blue, wispy white clouds cut through the sky, reinforcing the crispness of the winter cold. The three trees lined along the river that in autumn had once been full, red and brown, are now much thinner but not barren, taking on a dreamy shade of mulberry. The same smoke can still be seen rising from the buildings along the promenade, and the boat is there as well, only now, in addition to some human figures along the bank, there also is a white horse with a carriage in the foreground. The horse's saddle, the carriage, the promenade's mud, and the buildings are all rendered in the same mulberry as the trees, effectively dissolving any fundamental separation between nature and human business. Everything under the sun is bright and clean, bitingly so.

A further work in the series, finished a year later in 1880, is quite different from both of its predecessors. While remaining Impressionistic, it is considerably more realistic than the others. Over a subtle steel blue underpainting, there is a putty sky once again mirrored in the river's water. The same building smoke is visible as before, but the boat has vanished. So too is the horse with carriage gone. The focus is on the human activity, of which there is more than previously. A group of workers line the bank, handling timber on the charcoal promenade. The river trees on the opposite bank that Sisley in 1874 had shown in startling terracotta, and then in mulberry in 1879, are unremarkable this time, receding into a nondescript gray. Upon seeing this final version of the scene at Suresnes, it is fair to wonder to what extent the earlier works were perhaps romanticisms, more so departures from what was there to be seen, than straightforward renderings of it.

How an interaction between our emotions and our surroundings shapes what we perceive is a theme to which the artist would return. Exploring the role place has in forming our perspective is *Small Meadows in Spring* (1881), a work in which Sisley again turns to the delights of wandering along a secluded waterway path. While it is true that our mood can shape what we see, sometimes our surroundings are equally capable of shaping us. Such is the case here, as Sisley shows. Emerging from winter and so about to bud, trees line a dirt path through a grassy meadow along a river. A woman in her pastel blue dress stands alone in the foreground, perhaps pausing to look at a flower. A man sits on a bench, another figure standing across from him, probably some pair out for a stretch, enjoying the spring day. Things are crisp with the expectation of even greater warmth soon to come. This is not scarf weather; winter's bitter cold has passed. On walks like these when everything is waking up and renewing itself, we experience a freshness not only in the surroundings, but in our thought too, in our own form of rebirth that casts a crisp perspective on things, quickened and encouraged by nature's signal that whatever has been preoccupying us is not so intolerable as we felt, not so daunting after all. Like before in the Seine works, Sisley captures the connection among the earth, sky, and water, the big puffy white clouds that were billowing over Suresnes springing over the river here as well.

The nineteenth-century watercolorist William Turner, a personal influence on Sisley, as mentioned, painted works that bring forth the spiritual wholeness of the landscape, a oneness particularly evident in the case of the compact between sky and water. It is a holism held together by everything's being seen by God. For example, Turner in *An April Shower: A View from Binsey Ferry Near Oxford, Looking Towards Port Meadow and Godstow* (1842) provides insight into how the experience of a day's certain moment can serve as its own sort of microcosm of creation. When we ourselves are living righteously, friendship with God makes us feel worthy of the landscape's beauty, and allows us to feel a belonging to the harmony. The sentiment is not misplaced, for God has in fact transformed us into the first fruits of the new creation. Such is the melodious state of affairs at the Oxford meadow. As Turner shows, under the gaze of God, here one is just another creature alongside the ducks, swans, and cows. A walk along the river beyond the town center provides an escape from all the intrigues taking place among the dons in the City of Dreaming Spires. Conveying the simplicity of being, Turner has a mother in purple with a white sun hat holding a wicker basket, her back to us as she faces the river, and watches her children exploring a rowboat. One of her older boys, wearing a blue cap and brown jacket, leans over the boat's side to pull a fish off his fishing line. Standing behind him, another sibling looks to her two younger siblings, a very young boy and girl, the latter of whom appears to be offering the former a hand to come aboard. Two dogs are out with the family, keeping an eye on the situation. That the mother and children are out on the meadow alone without the father attests to the security of the situation, a safety originating from elsewhere. For as we see, they are safe with God onlooking. As for the river Isis (the local name for the Thames), while it divides the family from Port Meadow where a group of cows chew their cud, at the same time it serves as an accessible thoroughfare for the meadow's many birds. A mother swan ferries her bevy across the river, as a mother duck does the same with her raft. Across the way, a young boy and an elderly man with a cane (probably a grandson and grandfather) out walking their small black dog look on at the family. If there were any mistaking that each creature's activity plays a role in a mundane yet divine harmony, Turner includes a massive white rainbow spanning across the river, a visible token of God's covenant with his creatures.

Turner's Oxford landscape, which exemplifies God's covenant with creation, raises the question of how to understand that Genesis promise now. After all, it is, as the text says, "everlasting" (Gen. 9:16). What, then, is the ongoing connection between God's originating action to bring creation into existence and creation's continuation? Is the world to be explained by a temporal *creatio ex nihilo* having resulted in a world now conserving itself after being brought into existence, or is the world's continued existence sustained by God's ongoing direct action? If, as the latter view maintains, the world persists only insofar as it is continually sustained by God, is such preservation to be understood as a mere conservation, or is it a repeated and incessant action? For early modern philosophers such as Francisco Suárez and René Descartes, the question concerning the relation of creation and conservation bore directly on a further question, the important matter, for both metaphysics and theology as well as science, of how to understand the division of labor between human and divine causality. Very few would want to claim that God's conservation of the world is a kind of instantaneous action negating the reality of our own finite actions (this is the unappealing extreme to which the doctrine of creatio continuans was taken by Nicolas Malebranche's occasionalism, for example). Contrary to appearances, such a worry is not merely speculative empty. The stakes are clear when considered with an eye to the question of God's knowledge and human freedom. For if God is omniscient, how is everything not preordained, including our own actions, which it would seem are not free? In response to the worry, one might side with the sixteenth-century's Luis de Molina, holding to his doctrine of "middle knowledge": God foreknows our actions without thereby determining them. To be sure, theoretically explaining how this could be so is difficult. How God can know in advance what we will do, while our doing so remains free, has puzzled metaphysicians. But perhaps it is fine to acknowledge the question's fate is to remain a mystery from a theoretical perspective, while nevertheless practically affirming its truth, seeing as we all have the undeniable experience of acting freely countless times a day. This is not to inflate the power of our freedom. We are frail, unable even to secure our continued existence without God, for we are creatures only. That said, having been brought into existence and sustained by him, we can choose whether to exercise our powers to promote the course that God wants creation to take. If in humility's interest it always must be kept in mind that God is the Almighty, and not us, it is ennobling to comprehend the gift of God's investing us with the power to act freely. We are empowered, for we are free, but the freedom comes from God. As so often is the case, this one of our strengths, then, is a good reminder of God's own comparatively greater power.

Frailty is not simply human. It is cosmic. Paul says to the Romans, "For we know that the whole creation groaneth and travaileth in pain together until now" (Rom. 8:22). All things in this present world are passing away, preserved only for a short time by God. Creation, as Paul says, subsists in fallenness, groaning as God oversees the salvific work left to complete, saving as many of us as possible before calling this age to a close, the end of which will be to usher in the new creation. Why the early modern philosophers would understand the cooperation between human and divine action to be a legitimate concern for physics, and for theology too, is clear. But it is of concern for more than that! At stake is seeing for ourselves that we have been appointed a place between the animals and the angels, and that accordingly we are each meant to be co-laborers with God, individuals whom, by fulfilling our moral and spiritual role assigned to us, support the God's plan for creation's redemption. All eyes are to be pointed to "the new heavens and a new earth" (2 Pet. 3:13) that have been promised. For Paul, this means that what matters is recognizing Christ's pre-eminence through creation: "All things were created by him, and for him: And he is before all things, and by him all things consist" (Col. 1:16–17). Metaphysical questions regarding God's relation to creation and the relation between divine and human action are resolved simply by imitating Christ.

A part of human frailty is getting tired. At the well of Samaria, even Christ needed rest. The sort of refreshment we seek when tired depends on what we are facing. Rest is manifold. There of course are physical fatigues. But there are also spiritual and emotional fatigues, too. In response, sometimes it is necessary to take a break. Completed in 1887 at his garden pond in Giverny, Claude Monet's *In the Norwegian* explores one such rest, that of leisure. Like Sisley and Turner, in doing so, the master Impressionist underscores the harmony between nature and man. As Monet shows, the fact that we need breaks from work provides the opportunity for leisure, an interlude in which we take time to enjoy it, the moment being taken up for what it is simply for its own sake, free from any extraneous concerns that might intrude. No longer toiling, we strengthen ourselves by clearing our mind of tasks and setting aside our worries. There is a limit to what we can bear before we must rest, but this weakness is in fact the enabling condition for a spiritual refreshment. Work and rest, then, take on the form of a hermeneutic circle, each shedding light on the other, in turn strengthening us over time. Through iterative cycles of immersing ourselves in work and then turning to other things to take a break, we expand, our productive capacity enlarging, as we become increasingly capable of undertaking ever more in the wake of our periodic rests, sweet sabbaticals in which we savor the rest that sustains and refreshes us. Simple things like a walk, an afternoon at the park, or a day at the sea, will do. In this case, in yellow summer straw hats and draped in pastel dresses, Monet's three stepdaughters, Germaine, Suzanne and Blanche Hoschedé, take a small boat (a "Norwegian") out on the pond. The youngest, Germaine, casts her fishing rod off the front of the boat, her left arm resting on her hip, her eyes looking down into the water. Her older sisters sit comfortably behind her, the one in the rear of the boat watching her fishing line as well. This is a relaxing summer day. But whereas Turner and Sisley emphasized the sort of rest that comes with feeling oneself dissolved into a collective larger than oneself, here Monet explores a different kind of rest, one that comes with the tranquility of being secluded, as if protected by a secret. Monet conveys this specific feeling of intimacy by framing the scene to exclude everything except the figures and their immediate surroundings: here there is no big sky or countryside to be seen, but only an embankment with lime green vines and a boat floating on a periwinkle pond surface. Just as it is possible to escape our burdens by focusing on the vastness of something else, so also it is possible to find escape by focusing on the little details. Rest is as capable of originating from an attention to the familiar, for even what we usually take for granted is extraordinary, when it is seen without our worries and anxieties blinding us. Relaxation stretches time, not in the unpleasant way in which boredom does so, but in an invigorating way. Leisure time is a time that effaces us by dispelling our worries, leaving us less self-conscious than before. Fittingly, then, reflections of the three figures hover gently on the pond's surface, but the sisters do not notice, for their attention lies elsewhere than on themselves. As Monet shows, the everyday beauty around us gives us rest by delivering us from our worries. Work stops, and, no longer engrossed with our usual concerns, we are drawn outside of ourselves, set free by enjoying all the small yet sublime things God has provided us. If in Eden for Adam there was no toil whatsoever, today for us there at least is rest.

The typical juxtaposition between labor and rest is blurred by the work of Christ. Henceforth, it is now possible for work itself to be a form of rest, or at least to provide for its basis. How to explain this paradoxical work, this work that gives us rest? Where other forms of labor are always rooted in either material need or existential worry, the work that is done in Christ arises freely, and so it delivers us from our burdens. To work in Christ is first to lay one's worries down, and to instead set one's mind on what he has called us to do. There is no anxiety in such work, for in drawing close to God, we have no worries. To enter into the rest of Christ, thus, is to enter an experiential space whereby all of the subsequent labor we undertake is not exhausting, but rather renewed perpetually by the power of God always already sustaining it. Working through us, the spirit of God is a fount of power. The result is an inexhaustible work, a domain of action whose characteristic deeds draw their exigency from a reservoir of power ensuring that we are never incapable of accomplishing whatever we have set to do. If the truth sets us free, then the deeds that are done in Christ, in short true deeds, do not weigh us down and tire us out, but refresh us, liberating us from the yoke of fear and worry. Such is the immense power of God, even work itself becomes a rest, in turn giving us a peace that no other work can. The work that fatigues is that which we undertake alone, while the work that refreshes is that which we take on in Christ: "Come unto me, all ye that labour and are heavy laden, and I will give you rest. Take my yoke upon you, and learn of me; for I am meek and lowly in heart: and ye shall find rest unto your souls" (Matt. 11:28–29). In working what is good in Christ, our deeds work away worry, the anxiety of existence that would otherwise weigh us down is lifted. With God, our efforts purify us of worry, and our troubles wick away like sweat from our brow. This is divine work, work done in God, a work that lightens!

To labor in Christ is to abide in light, a light that not only guides our sight but lightens our inward load. Fumigating us of all worry, it leaves us pure, free of torment and dread. But it does not just empty us, for it welcomes in the grace of God. This is a process of refinement that leaves no dross. The result is a state of innocence. And although the means to achieving such innocence requires a submission to God that is an insult to pride (for pride sees it as a form of servility to an extraneously imposed arbitrary power above it), the humble one comes to embrace this way of existing's superiority to pride's autonomy. Humility is not without its justification for concluding so. For just as there is nothing pathetic about accepting help when we need it, so too there is nothing impressive about refusing it. If pride puffs us up, disrupting our natural equilibrium by inflating our opinion of ourselves, humility restores our balance, returning us to a state of lucidity. Domesticity is one place where innocence is at home. This innocence is the subject of Pierre-Auguste Renoir's charming portrait of the young Julie Manet. Titled *Child with Cat*, the work was commissioned in 1887 by her mother Berthe Morisot and her father Eugène Manet, younger brother of the famous modernist painter Édouard. Julie sits on a corner sofa, a flower print wallpaper behind her. The bangs of her short brown hair, with red highlights, dangle just above her eyebrows. In a stylistic choice the painter Degas would criticize upon seeing the portrait but Julie herself commended, Renoir has decided to give her a pronouncedly round baby face. There is something cherubic about it. On her lap is a big brown and white sleeping cat lounging contentedly in her arms, its eyes closed in comfort, its face crinkled into what looks like a delighted smile. Julie's piercing blue eyes are kind and gentle. This is the simplicity of childhood, a simplistic wisdom untainted by craftiness or ulterior motives that in its purity sees the beauty of things for what they are, and affirms and embraces them because of it. It is a look that is not weary, one that says yes to life, because it has not seen the evil and ugliness of the world that leads so many to cynicism eventually. Animals can be a good judge of character, which is why they have a natural sympathy for children. These are two gentle but sturdy beings, two creatures enveloped in a sense of God's security assuring them of their inherent dignity and worth. If the landscapes of his fellow Impressionists such as Sisley and Monet show well that God is known through the imposing beauty of the heavens and the earth, Renoir's portrait reminds us that God is also near to us even in the sitting room of a home. God's majesty can be unassuming, too.

In a continuation of what Renoir's portrait gives to understand concerning God's subtle presence in everyday human affairs, Camille Pissarro, the "Father of Impressionism," also does well to show the harmony we find in nature is not limited to that setting only, for the intimate linkage among creatures is also manifest in humans going about their work in the city. In line with Poussin's *Four Seasons*, Pissarro's compressed series of studies, undertaken from February to April, trace the evolution of the Boulevard Montmartre in Paris through sun, rain and fog, snow, morning and afternoon, night and day. With fourteen views in total, Pissarro captures the Paris street's identity in adumbrations, each slice serving as a testimony that, if one is attuned properly, God's hand is seen to be as much at work in the urban as the rural. Such was the insight that would reveal itself to Kierkegaard on his daily walks in Copenhagen. An abiding theme of his work is that a relationship with God protects us from a disgust with life, and guards against becoming embittered—it keeps us working, laboring in love to do what is to be done. To keep company with God, as he notes, is to renounce our own concerns, to renounce our egoism, and to instead love the ones we see. For while everyone needs companionship, it is only in renouncing our self-love that we finally discover there was always already an abiding community without distinction, one consisting of every human being, all of us living equally before God. Though many cultural critics have noted correctly that, with the Industrial Revolution, the modern city can be a place of exploitation, alienation, and despondency, a sensitivity to eternity places our ordinary temporal affairs in a different light, fortifying us against despair. In a chapter in *Works of Love* entitled "Love Abides," Kierkegaard comments on this harmonious solidarity among men, writing,

> When despondency at first wants to make you weak, so that you lose the desire to will rightly, in order then in turn to make you strong, alas, as despondency does that, strong in

the defiance of forsakenness; when despondency wants to make everything empty for you, to transform all life into a monotonous and meaningless repetition, then you do indeed see all of it, but with such indifference, see the fields and forests become green *again*, see the teeming life in the air and water stirring *again*, hear the singing of the birds begin *again*, *again* see the busy activity of people in all kinds of work, and you do indeed know that God is, but it seems to you as if he had withdrawn into himself, as if he were far off in heaven, infinitely far away from all this triviality that is scarcely worth living for; when despondency wants to deaden all of life for you, so that you do indeed know, but very faintly, that Christ has existed, but with a troubled clarity know that it was eighteen hundred years ago, as if he, too, were infinitely far away from all this triviality that is scarcely worth living for—oh, then bear in mind that love abides![11]

It is the city's "soul of life" that Pissarro harnesses so well. In the sole night scene of the series, a happy accord is struck between God's providence and our own activity. Everything, including the street lighting, is in balance. Newly installed electric street lamps give us a white light. A warm yellow light shines from the oil-burning lamps lining the cabs and the gaslight from the shop windows. The contrast between the artificial white light and natural yellow light is remarkable, not simply for its notable difference, but because they complement each other despite it. The urban scene is illuminated by the introduction of an artificial lighting enhancing and prolonging, instead of interrupting or disrupting, the life of the city. Darkness is a cover for evil, and here the play of lights throws everything in the open, making the boulevard a welcoming, rather than foreboding, place. If an afternoon stroll along the Seine or Port Meadow can be a refuge, so too is a night stroll along the boulevard. Night is no longer a place of total darkness, but a setting illuminated by light, a light that allows people to go about their business, or to enjoy a bit of leisure. Despite the many legitimate concerns associated with the unchecked proliferation of technology, here at least, the introduction of electric street lamps represents a positive advance against darkness, something that nurtures and promotes human activity, rather than attacking it, as many later technological developments have. With all the lights reflecting on the wet pavement, the street and its shops appear to hover, taking on an almost celestial quality. The dark blue night sky, dotted with stars, stretches out along the boulevard. Here the boulevard's lights serve to blend the earth and sky into one, not concealing the night sky altogether, but joining them together. The later excess for which contemporary metropolises are notorious is not present here, for the stars are still visible, not yet blotted out.

Visibility is no issue in a second work's view, *The Boulevard Montmartre on a Winter Morning*. Judging by the look of the barren trees, the boulevard scene in this instance was captured before the previous night scene, this one probably being painted in February. The electric lamps that had been visible only by their light are now detectable completely, their posts stretching high above the street. The people gathered at the base of the lamppost in the near foreground look small by comparison. That is not to say they look insignificant. Both the horse carriages rolling down the street and pedestrians walking the sidewalks are petite compared to the trees, lampposts, and buildings, an impression only further reinforced by the immense white sky above, and yet, nothing about the human activity below appears pointless or stupid. Things have their purpose, no matter how humble they may be.

A third work in the series, *Boulevard Montmartre: Mardi Gras*, shows the street transformed from a place of commerce, or even leisure, into pure play. Here, Pissarro shows us a scene of mirth.

Held annually since the sixteenth century, the Carnaval de Paris occurs after the Feast of Fools. Consisting of many processions leading to the Opera House of Paris, perhaps the most intriguing is the "march of masks." Beneath amber trees, a crowd lines the street in order to watch the processions. For an event that transcends social class, on this day, the regimented hierarchies and routines of typical work life are suspended, and people are free to join together to delight in the pure joy of being. The crowd, twenty persons deep, spills into the street, extending as far as the eye can see, an army of citizens united in the cause of forgetting the distinctions that ordinarily divide them. There is something eschatological about the celebration, a festivity that portends a day when all such distinctions will be eliminated for good, where everyone will finally be truly free and equal, not in some imagined socialist utopia of the future, but in the true end of history, the *eschaton*, the kingdom of heaven.

In the meantime, as we wait, relegated to live our days in whatever condition we happen to find them, we do the best we can, finding purpose in the daily work God has appointed to us. It is a fourth work in the series, *The Boulevard Montmartre on a Spring Morning*, that captures this spirit of lucid optimism. Winter is past, and it is spring now, the boulevard's trees bursting forth into lush lime green. The mud is gone, and the sky is blue, filled once again with those puffy white clouds that so enthralled Sisley. Looking at the boulevard buzzing, one can almost hear the happy sounds of the carriage wheels on the cobblestones, the sounds of voices, the chirping of the birds, all rising to enter the open window of Pissarro's corner room at the *Grand* Hôtel *de Russie*. Things in Paris, as anywhere, however, are never perfect, but if everything remains in a state of flux, the seasons coming and going, the day and night supplanting one another, the multitude of generations of people appearing for a time only to be replaced by new ones, it is because all such becoming aims toward a fulfillment in the kingdom to come.

The whole of life in this present world is itself a kind of great spring, a stage pointing to eternity, the endless summer.

That each of our labors has meaning, that we can rest in work by taking heart, is not an empty promise. It is eternity alone that endues everything fleeting in existence with its nobility. The trees and the mountains, the rivers and the oceans, the sun and the moon, run their course, every creature completing its task simply in virtue of its having appeared in order to be for a time. To be sure, nobody can envision what eternity will be, but if we can be forgiven for sometimes hoping that there will still be such things as the stars and the birds and the trees there, it is because their beauty attests to God, for it is of God. They are reminders of the Word who has spoken them into being. On the night before his crucifixion, when taken to the palace of the high priest for examination, Christ was challenged by the elders to demonstrate his authority, if indeed he were the Messiah: "Art thou the Christ? Tell us" (Luke 22:67). His response could not be any more direct: "I am, and you shall see the Son of Man coming in the clouds" (Mark 14:62). Christ's answer is prophetic, to be sure. At the same time, pointing our attention to the heavens, these words of Christ underscore the way by which we originally have all been acquainted with God, and the means by which we are reminded of his abiding presence, so long as we only look up and *see*: "For the invisible things of him from the creation of the world are clearly seen, being understood by the things that are made, even his eternal power and Godhead" (Rom. 1:20). Without doubt, the Word speaks through creation.

Chapter 8

Paul and the Philosophers

Creation declares the glory of God. In its own slight way, so also does the human voice. As the exploits of the prophets recorded in the Old Testament bear witness, a simple lone voice of righteousness, whether it be an Elijah or a Jeremiah, restores what has been defaced, retrieves what has been forgotten, reclaims what has been lost, sets things back on a firm footing. Is this not the human voice's noblest prospect, to join, and so attest, to God's voice? For if originally God established the world on its foundations only to watch evil invert that order by turning everything upside down, it falls to the voice of the prophet or apostle to once again put things right side up. Is the voice capable of such a great task? Is ours?

Such are the stakes described within the seventeenth chapter of the Book of Acts, where Athens and Jerusalem are recounted to have clashed directly at the Areopagus. In the wake of the resurrection, here two opposing wisdoms confront one another due to the mission of Paul, the emissary of Christ, the latter whom remains for the Greeks prior to that encounter the "unknown God" (Acts 17:23). Each of these wisdoms bears a distinguishing voice. On one side is the time's received wisdom, the conventional wisdom, the wisdom of the world proclaimed in Athens by the Epicurean and Stoic philosophers. On the other is an idiosyncratic wisdom, the wisdom of God, proclaimed first by the Jewish prophets and then in turn the apostles in Jerusalem on the day of Pentecost. Reflecting on the encounter recorded in the biblical narrative leads one invariably to wonder whether there is any commonality between these two wisdoms, or is all communication between them foreclosed? Contrary to a certain prevailing tendency accentuating the rift, while the disagreement between the two cities is undeniably fundamental, to be sure, it is not intractable. For, the true divine *logos*, the incarnate Word, is a power that enables a mediation between Greek and Jew. Or rather, the gospel of Jesus Christ opens a third way by dissolving both of these others, this new way being irreducible to either. As for Paul, then, he comes to Athens bearing a word compelling something other than a choice between remaining a Greek or being a Jew, for his message of "repentance and faith proven by deeds" (Acts 26:20) calls for something wholly unprecedented, in short, a resolute decision to be neither Jew nor Greek, but instead something else: to be a Christian, one of those individuals whom, as Luke reports, were said by their detractors in Thessalonica to "have turned the world upside down" (Acts 17:6). From the perspective of a world that has forsaken God and is plunged into darkness, the light of the gospel is an inversion, for it flips evil itself on its head in the name of good. Such is the power of the gospel that Paul comes bearing, the power to restore things to their natural order, as God had once intended but man had abandoned. Thus at issue is not a matter of either being a Greek or being a Jew, but a different either/or, one eclipsing any and all previous distinctions: either be a follower of Jesus Christ, or not. Old distinctions are moot, relativized by the revealed universal standard of God in Christ.

For his own part, Paul boldly claims to speak in the name of this absolutist doctrine, this new teaching that excepts nobody from its dominion. Upon hearing it, many deem what it says to be strange. And yet, it is not an exclusionary message. No doubt that partly explains what makes it strange, or different. The God Paul proclaims is one to whom everyone is equally obliged to worship, for, as the Apostle says, the people of every nation on the face of the earth are all "of one blood" (Acts 17:26). As earlier sections of the Acts record, the gospel's uncompromising absolutism is at the same time put in service of a fundamentally humanistic universalism, a spiritual egalitarianism so radical that its populist appeal offended the elitist sensibilities of those such as the Jews in Thessalonica, who, offended by its inclusion of the gentiles into the fold of God's salvation, accordingly rejected it. In arriving in Athens after being rebuffed in Thessalonica by the leaders of the synagogues, Paul meets further resistance, this time from among the local Greeks. Only here, in this instance, the elitism of the gentiles is not grounded in a misplaced sense of ethnic superiority as it was with the Jews. Rather, here the pride takes the form of intellectual snobbery. Paul cuts to the heart of the matter in short order, revealing such exceptionalism to be unjustified, by showing how its attitude of intellectual highhandedness betrays the very same ignorance it identifies, and rightly castigates, in the popular religion of Athens. Agreeing with the learned philosophers that it is correct to dismiss as superstitious the vulgar conceptions of the Greek pantheon, Paul at the same time nevertheless finds fault with the philosophical wisdom with which they attempt to replace it.

By the time Paul's journey led him to Athens around 50 CE, the decline of popular religion had been unfolding for many years, centuries even. Three centuries before Christ, for example, the Greek poet Aratus of Soli had taken aim at traditional religion in the name of Stoicism. His sole surviving work today, *Phaenomena*, a poem about constellations and weather signs, invokes the figure of Zeus in its opening lines. But it is not the familiar, traditional Zeus. Instead of an anthropomorphic understanding of Zeus as a personal entity presiding over the sun and stars, Aratus characterizes the Olympian god as an impersonal cosmic force, a divine Reason, or world-soul, said to permeate everything: "Let us begin with Zeus, whom we mortals never leave unspoken. For every street, every market-place is full of Zeus. Even the sea and the harbour are full of this deity. Everywhere everyone is indebted to Zeus. For we are indeed his offspring."[12] God for the Stoics is not the transcendent creator of the world, but a divine principle governing from within. According to Stoicism, then, the pantheon of gods, including Zeus, is not to be taken seriously. And if these gods are really mythical inventions, then the ordinary veneration of them are no less superstitious. To believe that the gods dwell in places constructed by human hands is irrational and contrary to the nature of the divine Reason, which itself dwells neither in manmade temples or shrines, but in all things. Such as Paul would find it is the Stoic view.

Needless to say, Paul's own message agrees in part with this demythologization effort, in that the gospel of Christ is also a teaching rejecting crass superstition and idolatry. Even still, if the Athenian philosophers see it as an oddity when they encounter it. In fact, it aroused their curiosity. As the text relates, Mars Hill, which at the time functioned as a judicial court, was also a space for intellectual discussion and amusement, a place where the philosophers debated one another, and shared stories of all things in the heavens and on earth. To come bearing "strange things" (Acts 17:20), then, as Paul does, would pique the interest of the city's intelligentsia, since such Athenians, like those of the modern European salons would later, "spent all their time in nothing else, but either to tell, or to hear some new thing" (Acts 17:21). Paul finds himself invited there for questioning.

A sizeable crowd is shown assembled at the Areopagus to hear him in Raphael's portrayal of the scene, *St Paul Preaching in Athens* (1515). Commissioned by Pope Leo X for the Sistine Chapel, the tapestry's near foreground shows Paul, cloaked in a green undergarment and red toga, standing on the edge of the court steps, his arms raised to the sky, beseeching those gathered in the courtyard before him to listen. A man sitting a few feet behind Paul watches intently, hand on his chin, pondering what he hears. There is no sign of either resentment or consternation on his face. He looks placid, receptive even, a fact Raphael conveys symbolically by the man's wearing the same green shade of undergarment as Paul. The two, at least to some extent, are sympatico. It makes sense that some in the audience would be willing to consider Paul's words earnestly. Intellectual historians have for a long time noted the fact that many Christian thinkers such as Tertullian, for one, were to find elements of Stoicism, its moral outlook in particular, congenial. The Epicureans in the audience would not be amenable to Paul's speech, first of all simply because it would sound too much like the Stoicism with which they were already familiar, and had rejected. For the Epicureans, life is about achieving tranquility through the disciplined cultivation of pleasure. Paul's stressing the imperative of righteousness would not be received well. When the Stoics encountered Paul's teaching, however, some of them immediately recognized the common ground. Their moral outlooks are similar. Virtue is sufficient for happiness, the Stoics held. And essential to the good life, they maintained, is the elimination of the passions. While natural impulses are of themselves innocuous, when they become disproportionate or are misdirected, the resulting excess leads to vice. Things such as fear and anger are therefore to be mastered, for they have no place in the life of the sage. Paul himself touts similar things: a courage that overcomes fear, a patience that subdues anger, a steadfast loyalty to the good that is ready to die when that is what is required of it. Wisdom finds virtue, a virtue that makes us free, for it is the passions that enslave us. Like a Stoic, Paul says in Galatians that the path to virtue, which for him means life in the Spirit rather than in the flesh, passes through the mortification of excessive desires: "And they that are Christ's have crucified the flesh with the passions and lusts" (Gal. 5:24).

Facing Paul is another man, also in that same green, his hands placed gently on his waist, his head slightly tilted in perplexity, as he listens calmly. Once again, the notable thing is that he indeed listens. Although there is no anger or disgust in his appearance, there is an unmistakable trace of concern, a worry evident in his hunching shoulders. By the looks of it, the philosopher is under a conviction. The general atmosphere of ambivalence with which he receives Paul's words is underlined further by a third listener, the most striking figure of the work, aside perhaps from Paul himself. In the corner of the right foreground, a young man with striking red hair and beard, again wearing that same green undergarment underneath an orange toga, kneels on the steps, and stretches out his arms to Paul, with a look of pure delight and veneration on his face. *This* is what he has been waiting to hear! For him, the riddle of existence is solved, the mystery dispelled, and the confusion cleared away, for God is indeed now known. In the work's background is a temple to the gods, its pillars the same green as the garments of the three men mentioned above. Is Raphael suggesting the presence of the Holy Spirit with this green? As for the others assembled in the court, things are different, for they show no sign at all of being receptive. Rather than accept Paul's news, they to varying degrees of vehemence reject it. In the open space between the temple and the crowd stands a statue of Ares, the Greek god of war. Raphael reminds us that Paul has in his own way come to declare war, for as a soldier of Jesus Christ, he opposes the worship of the city's false gods. To those either wedded to Athenian popular religion or its philosophy, Paul's message of peace, that all men are equal before Christ as children of God, and that everyone, Greek and Jew alike, are to set aside their former allegiances in the name of a God who has come to unite them as one, threatens their respective parochial ways of life. A man robed in white (whether he is an Epicurean or Stoic is unclear) rests his head on his staff, his furrowed brow indicative that what he is hearing from Paul, if true, represents the end of what he had taken to be true. He looks troubled, disturbed by the possibility that he has been wrong, misled by what he thought was wisdom into error. Another man accompanying him is even more deflated, his chin to his chest, and his arms crossed. Again employing clothing color to symbolize the figure's soul state, Raphael has the man dressed in the same red toga as Paul's, but without the green undergarment. This, thus, is an individual whose inner man—metaphorically represented by the absence of green—who for whatever the reason is resisting, rather than welcoming, knowledge of who God truly is. As much as the Stoics themselves decry the superstitions of Athens, they still remain superstitious. For the revelation of God in Christ establishes more than the fact that divinity does not live in shrines made by man (the Stoics had already concluded so before meeting Paul); it furthermore means that, contrary to the pantheistic conception of divinity to which they ascribe, there exists a transcendent creator of the world, and not just any sort of creator, but one who has involved himself intimately in the course of his creation, a God who above all commands that everyone, including the Greeks, obey. This is hard for some of the philosophers to accept. It is an unpalpable thing, because if it is true, their own wisdom ultimately is no less superstitious than the popular religion they had criticized for being so. Paul's proclamation of Christ demythologizes the residual superstitiousness of the Greek philosophical critique of its own culture's popular religion. As it happens, those listening are confronted with the unsettling realization that it is as possible to erect an idol in our minds as it is one of stone.

Surely, it is rational to suspend judgment where we genuinely do not know. In such cases, ignorance is acceptable, perhaps even unavoidable. Purporting to know what one in fact is not in a position to know runs the risk of inviting superstition. But when the truth has been revealed, and one persists in ignorance, what previously had been an admirable attitude of epistemic modesty itself becomes superstition, for it clings to an ignorance that has ceased to be warranted. Now the situation takes on a different complexion. What formerly was epistemic *askesis* starts looking less like intellectual humility, and more like willful blindness. Paul notes that such blindness itself leads to its own kind of ignorance and superstition. "Ye men of Athens," he notes, "I perceive that in all things ye are too superstitious" (Acts 17:22). Too superstitious in two respects. First, there is the superstition of the popular religion of Athens which falsely believes that altars and temples are the home of the divine. This is incorrect, because it is actually, we, ourselves who are meant to be the dwelling place of God: as he explains elsewhere, "ye are the temple of God" (1 Cor. 3:16), "for the temple of God is holy, which ye are" (1 Cor. 3:17). Second, then, is the superstition of the philosophers, who, despite rejecting the idolatrous idea that God resides in buildings or things made by men, persist in their own form of ignorance, denying the existence of the one true God in favor of an image of divinity they have fashioned in their minds.

With its central gesture, Giovanni Ricco makes this displacement of mystery, and its corresponding rebuke of idolatry, the subject of his *St Paul in the Areopagus*. Laying his left hand to his breast as a pledge of his sincerity, his right arm outstretched pointing to the sign about the unknown God, Paul directs the attention of the listening philosophers to the inscribed words lying beyond what is visible on the canvas. His onlookers sit in a semi-circle in front of four high columns shrouded from behind by drapes. In the court are three soldiers standing to the side, their conspicuous presence reminding us that, although the biblical account is silent on the precise nature of Paul's summons to the court, there is the real possibility that, if his words are not received badly, he might be punished accordingly. Where Raphael conveys the encounter's dimension of philosophical curiosity, here Ricco chooses to accentuate the meeting's implicit juridical, even inquisitorial, nature. Instead of Paul standing above the philosophers as before, Ricco shows the philosophers seated perched above a standing Paul. The discussion's appearance has more in common with a courtroom proceeding than it does a public debate. Paul, it seems, is on trial. In the middle of the seated philosophers is one man particularly transfixed by Paul's testimony. With a look of wonder and serene longing on his face, his hands prayerfully clasped together over his chest, he looks off into the distance dreamily, evidently struck by the magnificence of Paul's revelation. Like in the Raphael, it stands to reason that this enthralled figure is Dionysius the Areopagite, one of the individuals the biblical text says was convinced by Paul, and so converted. In a symbolic technique already encountered in Raphael, Ricco employs color to show that, for this new convert whose questions have been answered, and who embraces the ending of ignorance, the prospects of an existence secure in this newfound knowledge of God is seen to be as bright and vibrant a possibility as his orange and teal garments. The gospel has fallen on good ground, a receptive heart, for Dionysius responds to the call of God truly and purely, having "obeyed from the heart that form of doctrine which was delivered unto you" (Rom. 6:17).

Tranquil the scene is not in Mariano Fortuny's 1855 *St. Paul in the Areopagus*! Fortuny instead envisions a thundery encounter. A fiery Paul, his face grimacing and contorting in passion, bellows as he extends his pointed finger straight up to the sky above. A dark frock and red undergarment on, his left arm locked across his torso as if wielding an invisible shield, Paul makes for an imposing, aggressive figure. Everything else in the composition, including the other people, is washed out in beige and white. The group of sitting philosophers look like children being chastised by a parent or students by a teacher. One demoralized figure, visible only in the barest of shapes, can be seen looking glumly, his heavy head collapsed into his hand. To his left is another seated philosopher with deep lines of worry burrowing into his forehead, his hand on his chin, as he stares at the ground intensely. The others do not look any better, each burdened by the words they are hearing. Judging by their reactions, Paul is reaching the concluding stretch of his speech, where, having explained the person of Jesus and the resurrection of the dead, he says that God has commanded all men everywhere to repent. While the biblical text reports some merely mocked this warning, there is hardly any of that noticeable here. A few feet behind Paul, on the foreground's left, a soldier looking on at Paul and the philosophers has a wry smile, but it is unclear whether he finds Paul amusing, or whether instead he is taking a perverse pleasure in watching the philosophers all squirm. If it is an old rule of law never to ask a question to which one does not already know the answer, here the Epicurean and Stoics have learned so the hard way. Having initially invited Paul to tell his story out of idle curiosity, now they are not so jovial. For everything has taken a far more serious turn than they had imagined possible. While Epicureanism discounts the notion of an afterlife holding everything to be about pleasure in this life, and Stoicism insists life is about a happiness won through virtue, Paul takes things a step further than the latter, declaring that the only happiness truly worth seeking is eternal happiness, a happiness depending on virtue, to be sure, since we will be judged by God on the resurrection day according to our deeds.

Completed a century before Fortuny's foreboding watercolor, Giovanni Paolo Pannini's 1744 *Sermon of St Paul amidst the Ruins* is rather idyllic, actually quite charming. Pannini exteriorizes the pagan nostalgia for a past ignorance, and so accompanying innocence, one the philosophers in Athens feel stripped from them by Paul's sermon. For those like the Epicureans who wanted to take delight in this life's delights without fear of the gods, the days when it remained possible to do so by pleading ignorance of God was consequently the golden age, an age of play and enjoyment. Where the audience in most other works in the Areopagus genre are comprised almost exclusively of male philosophers, the scene here is different, with a number of women and children lounging about to listen. A standing mother holds a young child, the Roman archway behind her opening onto a huge bright blue sky of billowing white clouds. In front of her, a woman sits on the rock slab on which Paul is preaching, her feet resting on the steps. She looks up at him with an expressionless face, her countenance as lifeless as the stones themselves. Things are so languid, in fact, that a man on the work's right foreground turns casually to speak to an onlooker as he is walking away, his detachment suggesting he has more interesting things to do with his time than stay and listen. The man standing right next to Paul, probably Dionysius, does not look amazed either. None of the enthusiasm showing in the Raphael or Ricco is present here. And as for Paul himself, unlike in the Fortuny, for instance, here he is subdued and even casual, his arm gesturing vaguely toward nothing specific, unlike in the other paintings which show his arms stretched dramatically heavenward. If he appears nonchalant, Pannini suggests it is because the God Paul comes to declare has always already been declared by the heavens above that loom so large in this expansive scene. Pannini's rendering shows a Paul whose job is to iterate calmly what creation itself has already said. God resides not in temples or shrines, which is why the massive marble columns of the building towering in the background are not so imposing or impressive. They recede into insignificance, reduced to ruins by the time that ensures all temporal things pass away, above all the epoch of a world trying to sustain a plausible deniability of God the creator. In light of Christ's coming, no such denial is still possible. With the eternal gaze of God making its presence felt, now not only in the visible things of creation as ever before, but in the person of Christ as well. Pannini's theological suggestion appears to be that it is the preacher's task, not to disclose what has not already been revealed, but gently to remind everybody of what already has been.

Exaltation, jubilation, and hope, on the one hand, terror, dread, or resentment, on the other—the nineteenth-century American painter Peter F. Rothermel's captures this epochal moment's complex brew of ambiguity well in *Paul Preaching To Athenians On Mars Hill*. A portraitist also known for depicting historical events, his painting of the Battle of Gettysburg being his most famous, Rothermel marshals that eye for realism here. Things are light and ephemeral, almost dreamy, though still serious, not at all frivolous. Almost half the piece is a baby blue sky, the Acropolis off in the distance, perspective suggesting that it is nestled in the clouds. But as for Paul, he is down to earth. Dressed in a simple black garment, there is nothing flamboyant about his appearance. He is gaunt and pale, not completely detached like in the Pannini. Still, there is something wraithlike about his appearance, as if he is passing through. Camouflaged in the cloud above his head is the faintest of halos. The dozen or so listeners are also gaunt and pale, almost elfin. Most of them are women, not male philosophers, and they sit huddled together, practically draped over each other. At the bottom of the steps sits a solitary man in the foreground. Deep in thought, he broods, apparently chewing on his nails nervously. Can this pensive figure be our Dionysius? If so, it certainly is not the overjoyed, ecstatic figure customarily shown. And which, if any, of the female figures is Damaris? Is it the woman slouched on her side at Paul's feet, or one among the six women sitting together behind him? If Rothermel gives us nothing determinate to go on, it is to accentuate the very atmosphere of pagan ignorance which Paul's words mean to dispel.

The revelation disclosed in Athens changes everything for the Greeks, by above all challenging what to then had been their settled understanding of philosophy. They had searched for wisdom by seeking answers about the cosmos and themselves, only to find their philosophy splintered into competing factions, and hence consigned to an underlying ignorance. It is into this scene that Paul, who proclaims Christ, without doubt adds insult to injury, by deflating many of this philosophy's cherished questions, either by answering what it could not, or else showing such questions to be trivial. Does this mean, henceforth, that there is no continued role for philosophy? No! The surpassing of philosophy would only follow assuming one maintains a notion of wisdom that itself must be abandoned. For if the philosopher is the one who loves wisdom, but wisdom itself is of God, the true philosopher consequently is the one who loves God.

From this perspective that properly recognizes wisdom's origins in Christ, it is accordingly Paul, not the Epicureans or Stoics, who is the consummate philosopher. As for the once vaunted wisdom of the Greeks, this species of the wisdom of the world, it in fact proves incapable of attaining true wisdom, for it remains ignorant of Christ. Contrary to a widespread mischaracterization of the relation between the gospel and the state of Greek philosophical wisdom, Paul's proclaiming Christ is not an act decrying reason in the name of an absurdism, but rather an act highlighting the absurdity of the very Greek philosophy that took itself to be the paragon of reason but was not, precisely insofar as it remained ignorant of true wisdom, the wisdom of God. Of course, in his letter to the Corinthians, Paul acknowledges the fact that this message of gospel wisdom goes rejected by some, for as he notes, the preaching of Christ crucified is "unto the Jews a stumbling block, and unto the Greeks foolishness" (1 Cor. 1:23). But some do hear.

As for those who understood the call, they comprehended and embraced the spiritual significance of the words they heard. When Paul spoke, they realized this was somebody not simply there before them in Athens, but at once elsewhere, in Christ, somebody who therefore was not an emissary of any earthly city such as Jerusalem, but of heaven.

Chapter 9

The World

When communication is no longer possible with the world, for one is no longer of it, and when those who for their own part remain of the world have nothing to say because one's own life strikes them as an exasperating self-indulgence, a paranoid craze, an immature fervor, an arrogant and feigned idealism, when one finds oneself alienated because these others are offended, as resentful of one's indifference toward temporal things as they are unsettled by one's preoccupation with eternal things, embarrassed over what they see as one's ridiculousness, then the world is silent, and only God speaks. John, who eventually faced exile on Patmos for not fitting in, writes of this solitude when, in his letter to his friends in Christ, he says, "Ye are of God, little children, and have overcome them: because greater is he that is in you, than he that is in the world. They are of the world: therefore speak they of the world, and the world heareth them. We are of God: he that knoweth God heareth us; he that is not of God heareth not us" (1 John 4:4–6).[13] To be cast off from the world, divine isolation! Yes, always to be ready to speak the essential to anyone who would listen, only to find how preciously so few there are who care to listen, for almost everybody prefers to concern himself with anything at all besides the essential! So many others entirely sucked into the world's vortex of only apparently significant things and events (the hottest controversy, the latest scandal, the newest pressing challenge, the currently most perilous crisis), and yet so indifferent to their souls, so indifferent to Christ who has died for them, and who has called to them, and will continue to call to them, even till the very last moment they draw their final breath on this earth, to realize that everything that once appeared to have mattered did not, and that the one thing they thought did not matter did. Oh, so few who listen! Overcome the world in this way, and just go and try to tell somebody about it, and watch his eyes glaze over. If one truly has overcome, then naturally one will understand why this reaction is as it must be, will comprehend why others can with a shrug declare that it is time to grab a peanut butter sandwich for lunch, and that the story of this overcoming can wait. Then one takes comfort in knowing that if one were instead to tell of a trip one took to some exotic destination, then everyone would listen. Go skydiving and scuba diving and at least one finds an audience. Do something very extraordinary: return, say, from a conference in Davos on some or other world crisis, then one will have everyone on the edge of his seat to hear the tale! But overcome the world, and there will be nobody to listen, nobody to hear, nobody to whom there is to tell the story. How, here, in the face of this terrific silence, can John speak of an overcoming?

Overcome the world—invariably, it will be as if it has not happened, it will be as if nothing at all happened, since, for the world, strictly speaking, it did not happen, for faith in Jesus Christ is not another event that takes place within the world, but rather an event that occurs precisely outside of it, since it consists solely in the inward decision to renounce the world as the essential, and instead to treat God alone as the essential.

In Athens, as elsewhere, Paul witnessed the word of God, which renders obsolete cultural distinctions such as those between Greek and Jew, met with resistance precisely for that reason. To those desiring to preserve their established identity apart from the revealed God, to those, in short, as yet unwilling to die to themselves and to find newness of life in Christ, Paul's words are an inconvenience, an irritation, something to be either mocked and ignored, or maybe humored, but with a knowing confidence that the words of Christ are not what they proclaim themselves to be, not universally authoritative words, but just another item for intellectual curiosity to be examined and understood, another doctrine on a par with the other ideas one encounters in life. Paul was not the only one to face such resistance. As anyone who does so comes to find, dying to the world leads to a type of spiritual alienation from those who remain of it. Predictably, telling others that they must do so too does not go well! The experience of John illustrates so. In his own personal case, this alienation took the outward form of physical exile. Banished from society, he found himself rejected by the religious authorities, marginalized by those who purported to speak for God institutionally, for his presence was an indictment of their false ways, an incessant reminder of the unwelcome truth they were rejecting. To be sure, to let one's light shine does not mean those still in darkness will not try to snuff it out!

If in the biblical context there is truth to the adage that no man is an island, it is because even when one is set apart from others, whether geographically by exile, as with John, or merely socially by sanctification, one nevertheless is never alone, for one now is a member of Christ's body, joined to everyone else who has chosen to take the narrow way. Turning to the scene of John's island exile, we consider Nicolas Poussin's 1640 *Landscape with Saint John on Patmos*. In characteristic neoclassical style, Poussin blends the old and new worlds, the former represented in the island's assorted marble and stone ruins, the latter borne witness by the sitting disciple, who with pen in hand is recording his testimony, having been an eyewitness to the Son of God, in turn having seen how such a revelation has changed everything. Reclining by a toppled column in the near foreground, John is seen in profile, an old but strong and determined man with a thick silver beard and full head of hair. In the Book of Revelation itself, which presumably is what he is seen writing here, Christ's "beloved disciple" explains the circumstances surrounding his writing as so: "I John who also am your brother in tribulation, and in the kingdom and patience of Jesus Christ, was in the isle that is called Patmos, for the word of God, and for the testimony of Jesus Christ" (Rev 1:9). Poussin depicts the small Greek island as an ideal landscape, a picturesque scene of geometric proportion and balance. But such perfection is only relative. For the harmonious order, impressive though it be, is nevertheless subject to time, the passage of which, as Poussin shows, ensures that everything of human fabrication, no matter its ingenuity or beauty, is destined to eventually fade away. Here, however, the ruination of one order does not entail a slip into pure nothingness, but rather the advent of a new order, one that is immutable and permanent, it being of heaven, and not of this world. In short, the temporal order (as represented by the mighty ancient civilizations of the age) must give way to a higher, celestial one, an eternal order which has been disclosed to John through the revelation of the ascended Jesus Christ. In the scene's middle ground is a line of robust oak trees, just beyond which, in the immediate background, are an Egyptian obelisk and Greek or Roman temple. Further still in the distance, in the far background, is a mountain rising from the sea, the massive white cumulous clouds of the crystal blue sky hovering just above. If the beauty and serenity of the natural order surrounding him is not his focus, for his attention lies squarely on that which he is writing, it is because John knows, and knows better than anyone, that all of the earth's current or once great kingdoms, whether Egyptian, Roman, or Greek, are passing away, now definitively eclipsed by the one and only true royal kingdom, the eternal kingdom of God. His task, consequently, is not to enjoy the admirable surroundings of Patmos, but rather to foretell of what is to come. The absolute seat of power has been shown to reside, not among the courts and halls of the kings of the earth, but at the throne of God in heaven.

Although it may seem so from just looking at the Poussin, as we know from the biblical text, it would be incorrect to assume John is alone. For there are of course the angels. In a theme to which we shall return later in the context of the temptations of Christ in the wilderness, the Book of Hebrews states the presence of a "great cloud of witnesses" (Heb. 12:1) all around us, angelic hosts in heaven who watch from above, and whom can strengthen us in our times of trial should our thought only turn to them. The existence of these angels is inconspicuous, as they inhabit an invisible reality to us. For John, however, they are given to be seen. Toward the beginning of the prophecy he is given, John is shown a glimpse of the throne of God. Legions of singing angels surround the Lamb, worshipping at his throne: "And I beheld, and I heard the voice of many angels about the throne and the beasts and the elders: and the number of them was ten thousand times ten thousand, and thousands of thousands" (Rev 5:11). Such is the angelic activity to which Hieronymus Bosch's devout yet quirky painting *St. John on Patmos* (1500) alludes. In a departure from the historical reality, John is shown as a youth, his pale pink-hued complexion closely resembling his flowing cream robe. His head titled slightly skyward, his ginger locks resting on his shoulders, the blue-eyed John gazes at a circular, yellow ambiguously moonlike or sunlike object resting on clouds, the figures of the Virgin and Child inscribed in the middle. In the middle ground of the landscape is a hill, a sapphire female angel standing with her wings extended fully, looking on at John. Something about the scaling is deliberately odd, for while the size of the angel relative to the actual hill would indicate that she is gigantic, she looks more so like a miniature figurine, something reminiscent in that respect of a lawn gnome. The bizarreness is accentuated by the two figures facing one another in the near foreground at John's feet, a small eagle on the left, a fantastical half-lizard, half-bird creature on the right. The bespectacled human face belonging to the strange critter is rumored to be Bosch's own. Contributing to the strangeness of the scene is that Bosch situates John, not on the Greek island, but instead in what looks to be the European countryside, for in the background is a river lined with sailing ships, a tall cathedral off in the distance. Why has Bosch put John before what is more like the bustling port of modern Antwerp than the ancient, remote Aegean Sea? No answer is forthcoming, and so it is unclear, an indeterminateness that further deepens the work's peculiarity. A very similar work from 1525, *St. John the Evangelist on Patmos*, suggests an answer. Like Bosch, the artist Joos van Cleve places John before a modern sea port. Not only is the setting similar, so too is the figure of the disciple. A young ginger-haired John, mouth agape in awe, writes in the book resting on his knee, his attention fixed on the Virgin with Child, who this time stands within an oval apparition, a shape that appears less so to be any actual celestial figure, but more so a portal from another dimension. An eagle, the evangelist's symbol, is seen landing on the ground, its wings still spread, looking as if it might squawk at John. Down below the edge where John sits is a bay, the open sea separated by a peninsula lined with various homes and businesses. The physical distance from which all the activity is set apart from John creates the impression that it is somehow small and insignificant, that those down below are not privy to what truly matters, what is being revealed to John. However, if van Cleve's interpretation of the biblical scene is supposed to function as a moral admonition against idolatry by reminding us of the ultimate paltriness of our daily concerns regarding business and commerce, the overall atmosphere of the composition is too fantastical and whimsical to accomplish its task. Curiosity admittedly may find the scene amusing to look at it, for the work is charming and pretty in a generic way. What we see, however, does not appear to be what we know it attempts to render, for rather than looking like the supernatural intrusion into the ordinary that John's revelation is, the event appears instead to be more so the imagined scene from a story book.

A grander, more realistic work perhaps better befitting the event's magnitude is Pedro Orrente's *St John the Evangelist on Patmos* (1620). On first impression, one might believe John is sitting atop a rocky ledge overlooking the sea. On closer inspection, though, the disciple is at sea-level, the navy blue ocean waves lapping up against the shore. A few feet away, on the left near foreground, is a seated middle-aged looking John, his broad shoulders slouching in writing position, legs crossed, his bronzed face in profile, as he turns his head to look up from the page.

A celestial figure—whether it is Christ or Mary is not entirely quite clear—stands atop an orangey cloud, bright yellow beams of light shooting forth from behind the heavenly visitor. Once again, John is accompanied by an eagle, this one bigger and more imposing than those previous, its sharp talons latching into the rock on which it is perched, as it stares sternly out to sea. The only sign of human contact is a lone ship way off on the horizon, its white sail blending almost completely into the surface clouds enveloping a distant rock outcropping. Despite the strong wind and harsh conditions, John himself looks unagitated. Nor does he seem very awestruck by the heaven's opening unto him from the sky above. In a way, here Orrente's portrayal of the revelation at Patmos directly reverses those of both Bosch and van Cleve, for whereas the latter shows a John who is mesmerized, even overwhelmed, by surroundings that it must be said are frankly not so spectacular, Orrente shows a John calm in the face of violent weather and a genuinely remarkable supernatural apparition. Removing much of the extraneous detail that was present in these other versions, Orrente has hereby eliminated any element of curiosity, instead reinforcing the moral significance of John's encounter with the enthroned Christ, the terrifying nature of which is essentially missing in the others.

Gaspar de Crayer's interpretation, *St John on Patmos* (c. 1649–69), takes a similar approach as the Orrente, even more drastically reducing the frame of visibility, so that all that remains to be seen is a close-up of John, quill in hand, his companion eagle at his side, only the head of which is visible. With his face in profile, John's head cranes skyward, illuminated by a bright, but authentically natural, light. Though the scene is dramatic, there is nothing theatrical or quirky about it. In his left hand he holds an open book, the base of which is resting precariously on the table edge. While the look of awe on his face suggests he may well be paralyzed in adoration, his body in fact is in motion, his right arm cocked at the elbow as he reaches across his chest in an attempt to put pen to paper. John, of course, is told by Christ to record the prophecy he is shown, the illumination without which he would have been unable to imagine, and yet, in light of the magisterial beauty of the glory he is shown (the legions of angels, to say nothing of the Lamb himself), the revelation almost defies expression, since what is given to be seen far exceeds what any human writing could do justice. In a clear indication that he recognizes the powerlessness of his words to convey fully what he is being shown, he tilts the book upwards, as if the light shining down will impress, and so imprint, itself on the pages. That Crayer refrains from actually showing us what John sees, but instead relegates it discreetly off the canvas, is at once aesthetically and theologically sagacious. Appreciating that the attempt to render visible what John records as having seen threatens caricaturing the heavenly realm's beings, Crayer opts for aesthetic simplicity, reducing what we see to the strictly natural, thereby leaving the rest to the imagination. This aesthetic choice to keep invisible what John sees of heaven might be understood as itself furthering a theological statement, namely that God's greatness being what it is, the divine majesty so outstripping our finite powers of comprehension that it consequently exceeds our powers of language, and those of artistic representation too, better actually to honor those incomprehensible heights by only indicating, rather than try depicting, them. Thus, if in viewing Crayer's portrayal of John's revelation at Patmos we are left desiring to see more, is not this fitting? Would any appropriate consideration of what resides in the heavenly realm do otherwise than leave us yearning for the glory that is to be revealed?

Such a glory is so great it instills not just wonder but fear. Unlike many of the other works of the genre, Jan Massys's *The Apocalypse of St John the Evangelist on the Island of Patmos* (1563) highlights this awesomeness of the ascended Christ, the Alpha and the Omega. At the beginning of John's written record of the revelation, the apostle describes being struck down by the dazzling light, as if dead, at the sight of Christ: "And when I saw him, I fell at his feet as dead. And he laid his right hand upon me, saying unto me, Fear not; I am the first and the last: I am he that lives, and was dead; and, behold, I am alive for evermore, Amen; and have the keys of death and hell" (Rev 1:17–18). Fear not? In his glory, Christ is so intimidating a figure that he has even to reassure John, the disciple who had formerly seen him Transfigured on the mountain, lived and preached with him, eaten with him at the Last Supper, watched him interrogated by the Pharisees at Caiaphas's house, seen him on the cross, had with Peter seen the empty tomb, and in turn had seen Christ risen in bodily form for the forty days and nights before ascending to heaven. Yet still, even this same John fears! Massys shows the wise-bearded John running, the elderly disciple in full flight, in such a rush, in fact, that he has dropped his book. If Christ's instruction is to "Write the things which thou has seen" (Rev 1:19), that will have to wait, for John has lost his wits, and is in no state to write down what he is witnessing. Indeed, he appears scarcely able to bear what he sees. Whereas other depictions of the Patmos landscape typically focus on the sea, the predominant focus here is on a frightening sky thick with ominous red and orange clouds, and erupting like volcano smoke. As for the figure of the appearing Christ himself, he is faint and unobtrusive, overshadowed by the cataclysmic heavens.

In a striking departure from the dramatic landscape envisioned by Massys, the artist Diego Velázquez in *Saint John the Evangelist on the Island of Patmos* (1618) portrays a meditative scene. A young John in white linen is seen sitting comfortably at night, his steady hand jotting down the revelation unfurling within a small orb of light above in the sky. Reducing everything else in the work's composition to black, there really is not much to see. Velázquez seems to be suggesting that hearing is as essential as seeing. Whatever John hears, evidently it is soothing, for the scene exhibits the mood of a tranquil nocturne. Rather than show the wrathfulness of the Lamb sinners will face on the day of judgment, Velázquez's interpretation of the revelation on Patmos calls to mind the words from John's gospel, where, in the fourteenth chapter, Christ consoles his disciples, telling them not to let their hearts be troubled, for "there are many mansions" in heaven (John 14:2), a capacious place with ample room for anyone who truly is willing to enter. The work gently reminds us that if God is sure be angry with whom he will at the Apocalypse, it is only because those who spurned his mercy will have done so needlessly. If we love God, there is no reason to be afraid.

Spiritually speaking, John's exile can be generalized, so that Patmos is a metaphor for the world. The world is a place of temptation, an arena of testing, our time within it a duration in which we either succumb and conform, or else triumph and overcome. Invoking language similar to John, the apostle James speaks of overcoming. Temptation, he says, is not something to begrudge, but something to embrace, for when we are tempted, this is a blessing, since whoever endures temptation successfully "shall receive the crown of life" (James 1:12). To fall into temptation, he thus explains, is a source of joy, because in testing our faith, moments of temptation are trials affording us the opportunity to obey God, the result of which is to increasingly free us from lust and evil desires, and instead to draw us closer to God as we grow in grace. Loving God proves capable of transforming us, for if the royal law is also the law of liberty, this is so because obedience to God frees us from the bondage of sin. Sculpting us in Christ, refining us so that we conform to his image, faithfulness to God in times of temptation perfects us, leaves us no longer empty or lacking, but at peace, complete in the abundance of God's love.

Thus, there exists an eidetic connection between love and evil. Love is of God, and as for the love of God, it is to obey him, to say no to evil by resisting when temptation comes. Evil, by contrast, is that which indulges itself, and hence estranges itself from God in vain pursuit of its own desires. When accordingly John says, "And we know that we are of God, and the whole world lieth in wickedness" (1 John 5:19), his statement is true simply because those who are of God love him by obeying him, whereas the world is a milieu predicated on negating the will of God: for instead of submitting to God, those of the world hand themselves over to their own lusts. John says, "For all that is in the world, the lust of the flesh, and the lust of the eyes, and the pride of life, is not of the Father, but is of the world" (1 John 2:16). James states explicitly what John's characterization of the world in terms of lust implies, by observing that consequently "friendship with the world is enmity with God" (James 4:4), for in failing to submit ourselves to God, we must have succumbed to temptation. God, as James hastens to add, is not the one who tempts us, for God has no hand in evil. It is the evil one who tempts us, the Devil.

A range of paintings show how Christ's temptations in the wilderness are paradigmatic of our own trials. Hedonism, materialism, and egoism are the Devil's three enticements.

Completed at the turn of the sixteenth century, Juan de Flandes's *The Temptation of Christ* (c. 1500–04) takes the first temptation as its subject. Appearing as a bearded man with goat horns, the Devil carries a stone in hand. Christ sits on a block, his right hand raised as if to say "Halt!" Christ's expression is stern, almost bored, as if he is tired of the Devil's attempts to trick him. Although the stone looks like a loaf of bread, Flandes does not show a Christ who looks particularly hungry. If this is supposed to be a temptation, there appears to be little agony in it. Following the Johannine analysis of desire, the "lust of the flesh" can be understood to signify an insatiable hunger, a hunger that is never satisfied, and hence a desire it is foolish to indulge. As badly as we sometimes might crave something—in this instance, bread when hungry—it is always the word of God that remains paramount. Christ's reply to the Devil, "Man shall not live by bread alone, but *by* every word that comes out of the mouth of God" (Matt. 4:4) inverts the Devil's logic of need, by subordinating carnal hunger to the spiritual hunger for righteousness. Hedonism, which says that our highest calling is pleasure, is wrong, for as it happens, the greatest pleasure of all is to please God, something that often depends precisely on our willingness to forego carnal pleasure. James levels a related objection to hedonism, noting that it is self-stultifying, since to indulge the lust of the flesh is only to subject oneself to what proves to be a futile desire: "You lust, and have not [...] and desire to have; and cannot obtain" (James 4:2). Carnal desires only leave us hungry, for righteousness alone is what fulfills us. Consequently, better to hunger to be filled by the word of God rather than mere bread. Christ underscores the lesson himself elsewhere, when, in the bread of life discourse, he says, "It is the spirit that quickens; the flesh profits nothing: the words that I speak unto you, they are spirit, and they are life" (John 6:63). At the level of hunger, of desire, it is still God who is Alpha and Omega, for he alone can satisfy us. God is greater than the flesh.

Taking the second temptation as its theme, Ary Scheffer's *The Temptation of Christ* (1854) shows the Devil using a different approach. Rather than trying to manipulate our hunger into hedonism, as with the first temptation, here now the tactic is to incite pride and thus egoism. Having placed Christ at the pinnacle of the temple in the holy city, the Devil tempts him, saying, "If thou be the Son of God, cast thyself down; for it is written, He shall give his angels charge concerning thee: and in their hands they shall bear thee up, lest at any time thou dash thy foot against a stone" (Matt. 4:6). Scheffer's Devil is a nude, muscular human with wings. He stands beside Christ on the ledge, flinging his arms outward, egging on Christ to throw himself forward. Like Flandes who envisions Christ unperturbed, so too Scheffer imagines Christ composed. Turning his head calmly to face Satan, Christ raises his right arm, pointing to heaven, reminding his tempter that he derives his identity in the Father, not the world. One might be forgiven for concluding that the scene suffers from being overly rationalistic, that Scheffer has inadvertently purged the situation of its actual temptation by simply presenting things as if Christ's resisting the Devil is a matter of course. To be sure, Christ seems totally uninterested in meeting Satan's challenge, since, when one thinks it through, it really is offering nothing to gain. Why, after all, should Christ desire to prove himself to Satan, when, as Christ knows well, Satan requires no demonstration that he *is* the Son of God. The Devil is lying, for of course he knows exactly who Jesus is. And in any case, even if Satan were in genuine need of a demonstration, this would never change his negative attitude of Christ, for he would still oppose the Son of God as much as before. The entire notion of Christ's having to provide proof of who he is turns out to be absurd, a silly game not worth playing. The temptation lies, then, not in anything stemming from the desire to prove Satan wrong—it is already obvious Satan knows what he pretends he needs to see proved.

Instead, the temptation consists in lording over Satan the very authority Satan denies, in short, the temptation for Jesus is to exercise his power as the Son of God, power that Satan pretends not to know Jesus possesses, in the hope that, by galling Jesus into exercising it, he will have caused Christ to cede it. For if he is to demonstrate his power as Satan demands, it will be done, not at the behest of obedience to God, but purely in the interest of asserting himself. This is the paradoxical strength of the Devil's provocation (indeed of all satanic provocations): that it taunts the one it targets into lowering one to evil's level. For good to prove evil wrong in the way the latter demands thereby is to prove it right, since to do so is to become no better than the evil provoking it. Christ's response, "Thou shall not tempt the Lord thy God" (Matt. 4:7), submits itself to the very power Satan seeks to subvert, in turn reminding the Devil that, because Christ is indeed the one whom the Devil asks him to prove he is, there is no need to prove himself, to anyone at all, but especially not the Devil. If so much of evil originates in human pride, especially in the egoism that succumbs to the temptation of having to prove itself to others, Christ shows the foolishness of such self-assertion. God is greater than sin.

The tendency to understate Christ's agony in the wilderness is one Gustave Doré admirably resists in his work's portrayal focusing on the third temptation. Painted in 1865, *The Temptation by the Devil* shows a gaunt Christ in the middle ground. In a valley below is a town. The sun is setting, a yellow and orange hue hugging the ground, slowly dissipating into a serene blue above. Doré gives us a Devil who himself is a creature of the dusk, his kneeling outline facing us, shrouded in the shadow of the light behind him. Though his head and outstretched arm are both humanlike, he is noticeably more grotesque than in the preceding depictions. The biblical text itself relates that the Devil is prepared to grant all the kingdoms of the world, "All these things will I give thee, if thou wilt fall down and worship me" (Matt. 4:9). As it happens, Christ looks almost repulsed. Almost, because while not finding the offer enthralling, it is sufficiently enticing for Christ to have to look away, not in disgust at the glory of the world's kingdoms, but as a bulwark against potentially stirring the desire for them to be his. What makes the offer ultimately unpalpable is its condition: Christ is told he must first "fall down and worship" Satan. Stripping away the veneer, everything comes down to Satan's pathetic desire to himself be God. Christ's overcoming the previous two temptations showed that God is greater than the flesh and greater than sin, and this third temptation shows God is greater than the Devil. For even the Devil admits it, wishing as he does to be God.

It is the triumphant afterglow immediately following the overcoming of temptations to which John Ritto Penniman's 1818 painting *Christ Tempted by the Devil* is dedicated. As the biblical text recounts, after the Devil left in defeat, "angels came and ministered" to the victorious Christ (Matt. 4:11). Standing prominently in the foreground, a rock cropping beneath his feet, a cliff face behind him, a town visible at the bottom of the valley below, an illuminated Christ raises his left arm to greet a group of joyous angels coming down from heaven. His flowing white linen undergarment and red robe are both spotless, nary a speck of dust or patch of sweat to be seen. If there was a struggle, in the aftermath of it, Christ has recovered well, as he appears not to be the worse for wear. Upright in a wholesome light, Christ towers over a disfigured Devil who for his own part has been left cowering in the dark of the near left foreground. His face tormented with bitter envy, his skin red with anger, he flies away, unable to endure the sight of the peaceful, content Christ. If we look to Penniman's Christ, we see the truth of James' formula: "Resist the devil, and he will flee from you" (James 4:7). What follows is the joy of having held firm, of having grown stronger, of having expanded through the grace of God. Such is the blessing promised to those who are "doers of the word" (James 1:22; Rom. 2:13), the blessing of those for whom faithfulness to God leads to overcoming sin, the flesh, and the Devil.

Finally, is not such an overcoming in fact also a victory over death? In his letter to the Ephesians, Paul equates the world itself to a kingdom of death, for its ruler is Satan, the one who through hedonism, egoism, and materialism seeks to destroy us by severing us from eternal life. If, as John says, the ways of the world are not of the Father, this is because the world remains under the subjection of the father of lies, the one who promises gratification in empty lusts, glory in self-assertion, and satisfaction in power over others. The entire picture of man it peddles is an edifice of lies, for to live in the way it prescribes is not to live at all, since to be alive is to be alive spiritually, but to live in bondage to evil desires is to be dead, to languish estranged from God in whom is eternal life: "And you were dead in the trespasses and sins in which you once walked, following the course of this world, following the prince of the power of the air, the spirit that is now at work in the sons of disobedience" (Eph. 2:2). To be liberated from this kingdom of death will require an overcoming, the self-overcoming of dying to oneself.

Briton Rivière's haunting but moving *The Temptation in the Wilderness* (1898) shows this clearly. The landscape is utterly desolate. Where is there to go in this wilderness, which Rivière renders like a lava field? An exhausted, forlorn Christ sits on the igneous ground, feet pressed together, palms in the dirt, his head slumped down on his chest. This is a battered Christ, a real man who is at the limits of his strength, someone thirsty, hungry, isolated and oppressed. On the horizon is an amber sky streaked with red. Christ's white linen appears drenched with sweat, the heat symbolized by the molten sky, the latter of which for its own part represents the emotional tumult raging within the tormented Christ. Without the slightest trace of pedanticism, Rivière gets us to look to Christ by simply looking at his suffering, and thus to appreciate this suffering, to see the Savior's love, and all that he has undergone to redeem us. When the landscape shifts, and takes this inspiring turn, evil looks so ugly, so pathetic, in the face of Christ's beauty. As for our own suffering, it too undergoes a transformation, for we feel that it is capable of accomplishing its own overcoming. Christ's own hardest moments have shown us the way. There is no longer any deceiving us. Sin vanquished, death defeated, the Devil and his kingdoms are exposed for what they are. This is the power of God, and the self-overcoming it makes possible. We are overcomers: nothing now except we ourselves can separate us from the love of Christ.

Conclusion

Perfection

God commands nothing impossible. For, in any case, nothing with God is impossible. Even perfection, we are told, is possible. The promise of perfection is mentioned from the beginning of the Bible, occupying as it does a recurring motif in the Old Testament. In Genesis it says, "Noah was a just man and perfect in his generations, and Noah walked with God" (Gen. 6:9). Later, it is Abraham mentioned: "The Lord appeared to Abram, and said unto him, I am the Almighty God; walk before me, and be thou perfect" (Gen. 17:1). Though he too often is remembered for his transgression concerning Uriah and Bathsheba, the fact remains that David knew something of perfection: "It is God that girdeth me with strength, and maketh my way perfect" (Psalm 18:32). And it would be wholly remiss to forget Job, the one of whom God said to Satan: "Hast thou considered my servant Job, that there is none like him in the earth, a perfect and an upright man, one that feareth God, and escheweth evil?" (Job 2:3). God's promises to the perfect are as numerous as they are wonderous: "Mark the perfect man, and behold the upright: for the end of that man is peace" (Psalm 37:37), or again, "The Lord will perfect that which concerneth me: thy mercy, O Lord, endureth forever: forsake not the works of thine own hands" (Psalm 138:8). The extolling of perfection, however, reaches its clearest and decisive zenith in the mouth of Jesus Christ, where, in the Sermon on the Mount, he summarizes things plainly, as was his habit: "Be ye therefore perfect, even as your Father who in heaven is perfect" (Matt. 5:48). It is fitting perfection should figure so prominently in a sermon regarding faith. For does not it take faith to believe, truly to believe, that nothing is impossible, not even perfection?

Walking by faith, Enoch, too, in this way pleased God. The way lies open. To take such a way, to walk by faith, is to resolve to put this present world at once behind and beneath us: first of all behind, for like Moses who forsook Egypt, to so resolve is to set out for elsewhere, and hence, as a matter of concern, thereby also to place the world beneath us as well, subordinating its claim to what is higher. What now matters is the kingdom of heaven, and the God who has called us there. When this transposition takes place, afterward time moves on, as do we, but with an important difference, for our remaining transit through the world, unlike the one preceding it, is elevated, the time by which we pass through it taking eternity as its end. Existence assumes the form of faith, for it becomes a task of stretching forth, a perpetual exodus always in patience seeking after the heavenly city, rather than turning back to idle aimlessly where it had begun. For, any such return to complacency, as faith reveals, would be to hand oneself over to live again without hope, since the existence that wastes away apart from God, as faith now well sees, cannot secure the immortality everyone desires, but must instead only perish in the desert, the shadow of death, the place of despair, whereby the one who so dies does so alone, without God. As, then, for faith's own journey leading not to death, but unto eternal life, what sustains it other than the love of God?

What does it mean to perfect faith, to be perfect in our faith? Immediately, and for good reason, it appears the love of God above all will prove essential. Such is the teaching of John, who speaks directly of perfecting love by consecrating our time in devotion to the God who has called us from darkness to light: "Herein is our love made perfect, that we may have boldness in the day of judgment: because as he is, so are we in this world" (1 John 4:17). Such a task is one that lasts a lifetime: "There is no fear in love; but perfect love casteth out fear: because fear hath torment. He that feareth is not made perfect in love" (1

John 4:18). Univocally, all of those who knew Christ best say the same. Loving God is a task that perfects time, a task that gives time its ultimate bearings, a task aided by grace, for it requires our enduring patience. As Paul explains it, the task is that "we may present every man perfect in Christ Jesus" (Col. 1:28); "That the man of God may be perfect, thoroughly furnished unto all good works" (2 Tim. 3:17). James too: "But let patience have her perfect work, that ye may be perfect and entire, wanting nothing" (James 1:4). And, of course, Peter: "But the God of all grace, who hath called us unto his eternal glory by Christ Jesus, after that ye have suffered a while, make you perfect, establish, strengthen, settle you" (1 Pet. 5:10). Perfecting time by working righteousness in the time that we are given, this is the great gift the grace of God empowers us to do.

In doing so, nobody begins elsewhere than with mercy. As Peter himself learned in the wake of denying Christ, the full nature and power of God's love is revealed for the first time in his mercy for us, when we ourselves were still in sin, when we felt unworthy of such love, but then experienced it bestowed to us anyway. While there are many such examples we might cite of this merciful love, one biblical episode in particular stands out, that of the woman described in John's Gospel, who, taken in adultery and accused by the Scribes and Pharisees, Christ rescues from being stoned. The subject of many remarkable paintings over the centuries, including those of masters like Titian, Rubens, and Rembrandt, we focus on just one. The work to consider, *Christ and the Sinner* (1917), hangs today in the Saint Louis Museum of Fine Art, where it was donated by Morton D. May, the friend and patron of the artist, the German Expressionist Max Beckmann, who in 1948 immigrated to the United States. Originally completed after the artist's return from the front working as a medical orderly in World War I, the work is remarkable for its honesty. This, to be sure, is not a work shying away from the lewdness of the situation in question. If there is a tendency on the part of those who have contributed to the long genre of paintings examining this biblical scene to purify it of its indecency, and simply hurry on to the situation's ennobling resolution, that is not the case here. Beckmann shows it for the scandal other works fail to acknowledge it is. Unlike in versions which situate the woman in a regal court or impressive temple, thereby providing something to distract us, the setting before us here lacks any such orientation, for there is nothing to see but entangled humans, their cartoonish limbs and garish faces invading each other. On her knees is the fiery-haired adulteress, her eyes shut, her hands clasping Christ's robe. Lest we forget what she has just been caught doing, Beckmann shows her with both breasts exposed, her left nipple rubbing up against her bicep. If at first it may seem to be an eye-catching, if minor, detail, it in fact serves to highlight a spectacular moral point. For as it happens, it is not the woman's nudity that appears vulgar, but instead the ugly gestures and contorted faces of the surrounding angry mob. A man standing right over the woman turns up his nose, an accusatory finger pointing down at her, a smug little snide smile on his face. He clearly is amused by what he has seen, and is enjoying himself immensely, content that he is not the one being singled out for such scorn. His is a misplaced self-satisfaction, however, for as we quickly notice, the only other fully visible face from the mob is notably different. There is no sick delight here. On the left, the man in question looks to have his arm raised with a stone in hand. But he is not going to follow through, for his face looks downcast, even ashamed, his eyebrows raised, his whole face slouching, as if the skin were going to droop off the bone. What does this man see that his smug companion has not yet? Standing between the two men in the center is Christ, his back turned to the man having second thoughts, his body shielding the adulteress from the accuser's potential projectile. Christ reaches out to lift up the woman with one arm, his other hand commanding the would-be stone thrower to stop. Christ's mouth is closed, and yet the famous words he is recorded to have said echo on the canvas: "He that is without sin among you, let him cast the first stone" (John 8:7). Too frequently, Christ's saying is taken in isolation, in turn abused as an occasion for the commentator to issue a stern lecture concerning the importance of compassion, and of how it is wrong to judge others, and so forth. But this banal modern attitude that takes itself to speak in the name of forgiveness and mercy fails to do justice to what comes next. For having dispersed the crowd of hypocrites and delivered her from the stoning, Christ pardons the woman, and, not condemning her, assigns her what henceforth will be her new life's task, saying, "Go, and sin no more" (John 8:11). This mercy is no cheap thing, for it has intervened so fortuitously, so miraculously, to change the woman fundamentally, by delivering her from darkness to light, the light of a life lived in the love of God, and which knows the power of the grace responsible for having rescued it from evil. How exhilarating an event, to at one moment be facing an ignoble and certain death, only suddenly instead to be delivered, saved by love, and now in turn given the opportunity to labor in its service. To be sure, everyone's own conversion might not be marked by an occasion so tense as this, but in essence the change is the same. Such is the day of salvation, the day on which henceforth every day will now be lived in the hope that has been rendered possible by God's mercy, this hope that renews itself in the expectancy of the glorious light of God's eternal kingdom.

In his second letter to the believers in Corinth, Paul characterizes this dawning of a new day as being one of promise. A promise, he says, impelling us to perfect ourselves so that we might be ready to receive it: "Having therefore these promises, dearly beloved, let us cleanse ourselves from all filthiness of the flesh and spirit, perfecting holiness" (2 Cor. 7:1). God is to be praised for his mercy, our very lives themselves in turn a living sacrifice to that gift, our bodies instruments of righteousness, our hearts perfecting their praise through the power of the grace incessantly flooding them, everything within us concealing no shadow of turning, now held steadfast in the open light of Almighty God's love. If to be perfect is to be complete, the absence of all lack here at issue consists in a felt wholeness impossible apart from the fullness only life in Christ gives. This is holiness. As anyone who assumes the task of seeking it accordingly comes to find, God, who has made us to find him, makes such abundance not just possible, but desirable. With the author of Ecclesiasticus, one comes in time to experience God's faithfulness: "All the works of the Lord are exceedingly good, and whatsoever he commands shall be accomplished in due season" (Ecclus. XXXIX.16). All things are possible in Christ. And for this reason, praise is man's vocation.

Notes

1 See Emmanuel Falque, *The Metamorphosis of Finitude: An Essay on Birth and Resurrection*, trans. George Hughes (New York: Fordham University Press, 2012).

2 Seneca, *Letters from a Stoic: Epistulae Morales Ad Lucilium*, XV, trans. Robin Campbell (London: Penguin Classics, 1969), 62.

3 Seneca, *Letters from a Stoic*, 102.

4 Ibid.

5 Tertullian, "On the Resurrection of the Flesh," in *The Ante-Nicene Fathers: The Writings of the Fathers down to A.D. 325*, volume three, eds. Alexander Roberts and James Donaldson (Grand Rapids, MI: Wm. B. Eerdmans Publishing Company, 1957), 553.

6 Ibid.

7 Richard T. Neer, "Poussin, Titian and Tradition: *The Birth of Bacchus* and the genealogy of images," *Word & Image: A Journal of Verbal/Visual Enquiry* 18 (2): 2002, 167–181.

8 Neer, "Poussin, Titian and Tradition," 169.

9 Friedrich Nietzsche, *On the Genealogy of Morals*, trans. Walter Kaufman (New York: Random House, 1989), 66.

10 For the Ancients, wisdom was the paradigm model for self-knowledge. Beginning with the Moderns, there has been a shift instead to a paradigm of authenticity. The French philosopher Claude Romano explores the distinction in *La Liberté intérieure: Une esquisse* (Paris: Hermann, 2020).

11 Søren Kierkegaard, *Works of Love*, trans. Howard V. Hong and Edna H. Hong (Princeton, New Jersey: Princeton University Press, 1995), 300–01.

12 The poem, translated by G.R. Meir, can be accessed online here: http://www.theoi.com/Text/AratusPhaenomena.html

13 The concept of the world is not without history. Following

the illuminating schema provided by the French intellectual historian Rémi Brague, we may identify four models of the world in Antiquity: the Platonic, the Epicurean, the Abrahamic, and the Gnostic. To some degree, they all persisted in one form or another through the Medieval period, until gradually receding in the Modern period, when the world increasingly ceased to be experienced as an ethically ordered whole suffused with value, but instead as a space of blind causal forces. As Brague explains in *The Wisdom of the World* (2003), each of these Ancient models can be understood in light of its view of the world's value and interest. On the conception offered by Plato's *Timaeus*, the cosmos is what is best, and knowledge of it allows us to reach the fulfillment of our humanity. Man is good, and so is the world, states of affairs Brague terms "anthropomorphic optimism" and "cosmological optimism," respectively. According to Epicureanism, the world is not good, yet neither is it bad, but merely neutral, and thus it largely is a matter of moral indifference, though theoretical knowledge of it can be reassuring. For the Abrahamic traditions, the world is good, for it was created by a good God, and knowledge of it is good too, since cosmic knowledge leads to knowledge of the Creator. Finally, for the Gnostics, the world is evil, and knowledge of it is useless, since the only worthwhile knowledge is that which allows us to escape the world (2003, 70). Brague, justifiably, is concerned with distinguishing Christianity from Gnosticism, and consequently he underscores that the former holds the world to be "very good" (Gen. 1:31), whereas the latter does not. Of course, as he acknowledges, it must be borne in mind that the New Testament letters do frequently characterize the world as being evil. How, then, to avoid the contradiction that seems to result: how, in short, is it possible to accommodate the Pauline and

Johannine statements that the world is evil, while also maintaining (contrary to Gnosticism's cosmic pessimism) that the world in fact is good? To resolve the tension, it is necessary to make a distinction. The world can mean different things depending on the context. When it signifies creation (or "the heavens and the earth" — what we today call nature), the world is understood to be good. When instead it signifies the milieu of everyday human affairs, the world is understood to be evil, for it is plagued by sinfulness, governed as it is by ungodly individual desires, unjust systems, and corrupt institutions. Such a distinction raises a further question. Is there, in turn, one single overarching totality encompassing both of these senses of the world? Approaching the question from a different set of concerns, the philosopher Markus Gabriel has contended that the concept of the world as a whole (a view he calls "metaphysical"), one on which the world is understood as "any kind of unrestricted or overall totality, be it the totality of existence, the totality of what there is, the totality of objects, the whole of beings, or the totality of facts or states of affairs," or what "usually is meant to designate the ultimate, all-encompassing unity or entity," (2003, 187) denotes something that does not exist. For an explanation and defense of this "no-world-view," see his *Fields of Sense: A New Realist Ontology* (2015). Despite denying the reality of any all-encompassing totality, Gabriel's thesis that "The world does not exist" (2015, 7) is nevertheless compatible with the second biblical sense of the world, the one for us at issue: namely, the sense in which it means the everyday sinful milieu of human affairs.

Works Cited

Aratus of Soli. 2015. "Phaenomena," in *Eratosthenes and Hyginus Constellation Myths*. Trans. Robin Hard. (Oxford: Oxford University Press).

Brague, Rémi. 2003. *The Wisdom of the World: The Human Experience of the Universe in Western Thought*. Trans. Teresa Lavender Fagan. (Chicago: Chicago University Press).

Falque, Emmanuel. 2012. *The Metamorphosis of Finitude: An Essay on Birth and Resurrection*. Trans. George Hughes. (New York: Fordham University Press).

Gabriel, Markus. 2015. *Fields of Sense: A New Realist Ontology*. (Edinburgh University Press).

Kierkegaard, Søren. 1995. *Works of Love*. Trans. Howard V. Hong and Edna H. Hong. (Princeton, New Jersey: Princeton University Press).

Neer, Richard. "Poussin, Titian and Tradition: *The Birth of Bacchus* and the genealogy of images," *Word & Image: A Journal of Verbal/Visual Enquiry* 18 (2): 2002, 167–181.

Nietzsche, Friedrich. 1989. *On the Genealogy of Morals*. Trans. Walter Kaufman. (New York: Random House).

Romano, Claude. 2020. *La Liberté intérieure: Une esquisse*. (Paris: Hermann).

Seneca. 1969. *Letters from a Stoic: Epistulae Morales Ad Lucilium*, XV. Trans. Robin Campbell. (London: Penguin Classics).

Tertullian, 1957. "On the Resurrection of the Flesh," in *The Ante-Nicene Fathers: The Writings of the Fathers down to A.D. 325*, volume three. Eds. Alexander Roberts and James Donaldson. (Grand Rapids, MI: Wm. B. Eerdmans Publishing Company).

Artworks

Max Beckmann, *Christ and the Sinner*, 1917. Oil on canvas. 58.8 by 49.9 in. Saint Louis Museum of Art.

Giovanni Bellini, *Drunkenness of Noah*, 1515. Oil on canvas. 40.5 by 61.8 in. Besançon, Musée des Beaux-Arts et d'Archéologie.

Ferdinand Bol, *Elijah Fed by an Angel*, c. 1660–63. Oil on canvas, 53.1 by 60.2 in. Private Collection.

Eugène Bordin, *The Port of Bordeaux*, 1874. Oil on canvas, 15.7 by 25.7 in. Edinburgh, National Galleries of Scotland.

Hieronymus Bosch, *St. John on Patmos*, 1500. Oil on canvas, 25 by 17 in. Staatliche Museen.

Adriaen Brouwer, *Peasants Brawling over Cards*, 1630. Oil on oak, 10.4 by 13.5 in. Dresden, Staatliche Kunstsammlungen.

— — —. *Tavern Scene*, 1635. Oil on oak, 18.9 by 26.4 in. London, National Gallery.

Michelangelo Merisi da Caravaggio, *Conversion on the Way to Damascus*, 1600–01. Oil on canvas, 91 by 69 in. Rome, Parish Basilica of Santa Maria del Popolo.

— — —. *The Conversion of Saint Paul*, 1600-01. Oil on canvas, 93 by 74 in. Rome, Odescalchi Balbi Collection.

— — —. *The Incredulity of Saint Thomas*, 1601–02. Oil on canvas, 42 by 57 in. Potsdam, Sanssouci Picture Gallery.

— — —. *Narcissus*. 1597–99. Oil on canvas, 43.3 by 36.2 in. Rome, Galleria Nazionale d'Arte Antic.

Antonio Ciseri, *Ecce Homo*, 1891. Oil on canvas, 115 by 149.6 in. Florence, Galleria dell'Arte Moderna, Palazzo Pitti.

Joos van Cleve, *St. John the Evangelist on Patmos*, 1525. Oil on panel, 28.3 by x 29.1 in. University of Michigan Museum of Art.

Gaspar de Crayer, *St John on Patmos*, c. 1649–69. Oil on canvas, 50.9 by 39.6 in. Ghent, Museum of Fine Arts.

Paul Gustave Doré, *Prophet Elijah Fed by an Angel*, 1866.

Engraving in wood. In *The Doré Bible Illustrations* (New York: Dover Publications, 1974).

— — — . *The Temptation by the Devil*, 1865.

Juan Antonio Frias y Escalante, *An Angel Awakens the Prophet Elijah*, 1667. Oil on wood, 19.7 by 13.3. in. Berlin, Gemäldegalerie.

Juan de Flandes, The Temptation of Christ, c. 1500–04.

Mariano Fortuny, *St. Paul in the Areopagus*, 1855.

Jean-Honoré Fragonard, *The Swing*, 1767. Oil on canvas, 31.8 by 25.3 in. London, Wallace Collection.

Gustave Guillaumet, The Sahara, or the Desert, 1867. Oil on canvas, 43.3 by 78.7 in. Paris, Musée d'Orsay.

Claude Lorrain, *Seaport with the Embarkation of the Queen of Sheba*, 1648. Oil on canvas, 58.7 by 77.4 in. London, National Gallery.

Francesco Maggiotto, *The Feeding of Elijah by the Angel*, 1780. Oil on canvas. Venice, San Giovanni in Bragora.

Jan Massys, *The Apocalypse of St John the Evangelist on the Island of Patmos*, 1563. Oil on oak, 46.1 by 57.8 in.

Claude Monet, *In the Norwegian*, 1887. Oil on canvas, 38.6 by 51.6 in. Paris, Musée d'Orsay.

Alessandro Bonvicino Moretto, *Elijah Visited by an Angel*, c. 1534. Brescia, Chiesa di San Giovanni Evangelista.

Edvard Munch, The Dance of Life, 1899–1900. Oil on canvas, 50.7 by 75.1 in. Oslo, National Museum of Art, Architecture and Design.

— — — . *Kiss by the Window*, 1892. Oil on canvas, 28.7 by 36.2 in. Oslo, National Museum of Art, Architecture and Design.

— — — . *Night in Saint-Cloud*, 1890. Oil on canvas, 25.3 by 21.2 in. Oslo, National Museum of Art, Architecture and Design.

Pedro Orrente, *St John the Evangelist on Patmos*, 1620.

Adriaen van Ostade, *Drunkards in a Tavern*, 1640. Oil on panel, 16.5 by 22.5 in. San Francisco, Legion of Honor.

Giovanni Paolo Pannini, *Sermon of St Paul amidst the Ruins*, 1744. Oil on canvas, 25.1 by 32.8 in. St. Petersburgh, Hermitage Museum.

John Ritto Penniman, *Christ Tempted by the Devil*, 1818. Oil on panel, 23.6 by 32 in. Smithsonian American Art Museum.

Camille Pissarro, *The Boulevard Montmartre at Night*, 1897. Oil on canvas, 30 by 25.5 in. London, The National Gallery.

———. *The Boulevard Montmartre: Mardi Gras*, 1897. Oil on canvas, 23.7 by 31.4 in. Los Angeles, Hammer Museum.

———. *The Boulevard Montmartre on a Spring Morning*, 1897. Oil on canvas, 25.6 by 31.9 in. London, The Courtauld Institute of Art.

———. *The Boulevard Montmartre on a Winter Morning*, 1897. Oil on canvas, 25.5 by 32 in. New York, The Metropolitan Museum of Art.

———. *The Adoration of the Golden Calf*, 1663–64. Oil on canvas, 60.4 by 83.4 in. London, National Gallery.

———. *The Birth of Bacchus*, 1657. Oil on canvas, 48 by 70.5 in. Cambridge, Fogg Art Museum.

———. *Landscape with Saint John on Patmos*, 1640. Oil on canvas, 39.5 by 53.7 in. Art Institute Chicago.

———. *Spring or the Earthly Paradise*, 1660–64. Oil on canvas, 46.1 by 63 in. Paris, The Louvre.

Raphael, *St Paul Preaching in Athens (Acts 17:16–34)*, 1515. Tapestry, 12.7 by 14.4 ft. London, Victoria and Albert Museum.

Rembrandt, *Christ before Pilate (Ecce Homo)*, 1634. Oil on paper mounted onto canvas, 21.4 in by 17.5 in. London, National Gallery.

Pierre-Auguste Renoir, *Child with Cat*, 1887. Oil on canvas, 25.6 by 21.2 in. Paris, Musée d'Orsay.

Giovanni Ricco, *St Paul in the Areopagus*, Oil on canvas. Parma, National Gallery.

Briton Rivière, *The Temptation in the Wilderness*, 1898. Oil on canvas, 46 by 74.4 in. London, Guildhall Art Gallery.

Auguste Rodin, *Fugitive Love*, 1887. Marble, bronze, 17.7 by 19.6 by 11.7 in. Mexico City, Museo Soumaya.

———. *The Gates of Hell*, 1887. High relief and plaster, 250 by

157.5 by 37 in. Paris, Musée d'Orsay

— — — . *Thinker*, 1903. Bronze, 70.9 by 38.6 by 57.1 in. Paris, Musée Rodin.

— — — . *The Three Shades*, 1886. Bronze, 78 in. San Francisco, Legion of Honor.

Salvator Rosa, *Port Marina*, 1640. Oil on canvas, 28.3 by 52 in.

— — — . *Witches at their Incantations*, 1647. Oil on canvas, 28.3 by 52 in. London, National Gallery.

Peter F. Rothermel, *Paul Preaching to Athenians On Mars Hill*, c. 1866.

Peter Paul Rubens, *Flagellation of Christ*, 1617. Oil on plywood, 14.6 by 13.8 in. Antwerp, Belgium, Church of St. Paul.

— — — . *The Tribute Money*, 1612–14. Oil on canvas, 56.8 by 74.8 in. San Francisco, Legion of Honor.

Ary Scheffer, *The Temptation of Christ*, 1854. 87.6 by 59.7 in. Liverpool, Walker Art Gallery.

Alfred Sisley. *The Seine at Suresnes*, 1880. Oil on canvas, 25.7 by 18.3 in. Edinburg, National Galleries of Scotland.

— — — . *His at Suresnes*, 1879. Oil on canvas, 25.6 by 19.7 in. Private Collection.

— — — . *The Seine at Suresnes*, 1877. Oil on canvas, 23.8 by 28.9 in. Paris, Musée d'Orsay.

— — — . *The Seine at Suresnes*, 1874. Oil on canvas, 15 by 11 in. Private collection.

Titian, *The Bacchanal of the Andrians*, 1518-19. Oil on canvas, 69 by 76 in. Madrid, Museo del Prado.

William Turner, *An April Shower: A View from Binsey Ferry Near Oxford, Looking Towards Port Meadow and Godstow*, 1842. Oil on canvas, 17.9 by 27 in. Art Institute of Chicago.

Diego Velázquez, *Saint John the Evangelist on the Island of Patmos*, c. 1618. Oil on canvas, 53.3 by 40.2 in. London, National Gallery.

About the Author

Steven DeLay is an Old Member of Christ Church, University of Oxford, UK. The author of *Before God: Exercises in Subjectivity* (Rowman and Littlefield: 2020) and *Phenomenology in France: A Philosophical and Theological Introduction* (Routledge: 2019), he is also the editor of *Life above the Clouds: Philosophy in the Films of Terrence Malick* (SUNY: 2022), and editor of the series of online essays, "Finding Meaning in the Age of Nihilism," at *3:16 AM*.

CHRISTIAN ALTERNATIVE
BOOKS

THE NEW OPEN SPACES

Throughout the two thousand years of Christian tradition there
have been, and still are, groups and individuals that exist in
the margins and upon the edge of faith. But in Christianity's
contrapuntal history it has often been these outcasts and
pioneers that have forged contemporary orthodoxy out
of former radicalism as belief evolves to engage with and
encompass the ever-changing social and scientific realities. Real
faith lies not in the comfortable certainties of the Orthodox,
but somewhere in a half-glimpsed hinterland on the dirt track
to Emmaus, where the Death of God meets the Resurrection,
where the supernatural Christ meets the historical Jesus,
and where the revolution liberates both the oppressed and
the oppressors.

Welcome to Christian Alternative... a space at the edge where
the light shines through.
If you have enjoyed this book, why not tell other readers by
posting a review on your preferred book site.

Recent bestsellers from Christian Alternative are:

Bread Not Stones
The Autobiography of An Eventful Life
Una Kroll
The spiritual autobiography of a truly remarkable woman
and a history of the struggle for ordination in the Church of
England.
Paperback: 978-1-78279-804-0 ebook: 978-1-78279-805-7

The Quaker Way
A Rediscovery
Rex Ambler
Although fairly well known, Quakerism is not well understood.
The purpose of this book is to explain how Quakerism works as
a spiritual practice.
Paperback: 978-1-78099-657-8 ebook: 978-1-78099-658-5

Blue Sky God
The Evolution of Science and Christianity
Don MacGregor
Quantum consciousness, morphic fields and blue-sky
thinking about God and Jesus the Christ.
Paperback: 978-1-84694-937-1 ebook: 978-1-84694-938-8

Celtic Wheel of the Year
Tess Ward
An original and inspiring selection of prayers combining
Christian and Celtic Pagan traditions, and interweaving their
calendars into a single pattern of prayer for every morning
and night of the year.
Paperback: 978-1-90504-795-6

Christian Atheist
Belonging without Believing
Brian Mountford
Christian Atheists don't believe in God but miss him: especially
the transcendent beauty of his music, language, ethics, and
community.
Paperback: 978-1-84694-439-0 ebook: 978-1-84694-929-6

Compassion Or Apocalypse?
A Comprehensible Guide to the Thoughts of René Girard
James Warren
How René Girard changes the way we think about God and the
Bible, and its relevance for our apocalypse-threatened world.
Paperback: 978-1-78279-073-0 ebook: 978-1-78279-072-3

Diary Of A Gay Priest
The Tightrope Walker
Rev. Dr. Malcolm Johnson
Full of anecdotes and amusing stories, but the Church is still a
dangerous place for a gay priest.
Paperback: 978-1-78279-002-0 ebook: 978-1-78099-999-9

Do You Need God?
Exploring Different Paths to Spirituality Even For Atheists
Rory J.Q. Barnes
An unbiased guide to the building blocks of spiritual belief.
Paperback: 978-1-78279-380-9 ebook: 978-1-78279-379-3

Readers of ebooks can buy or view any of these bestsellers by clicking on the live link in the title. Most titles are published in paperback and as an ebook. Paperbacks are available in traditional bookshops. Both print and ebook formats are available online.

Find more titles and sign up to our readers' newsletter at
http://www.johnhuntpublishing.com/christianity
Follow us on Facebook at
https://www.facebook.com/ChristianAlternative